CHILDREN'S
ENCYCLOPEDIA
OF QUESTIONS
AND ANSWERS

Lisa Regan

ARCTURUS

ARCTURUS

This edition published in 2022 by Arcturus Publishing Limited
26/27 Bickels Yard, 151–153 Bermondsey Street,
London SE1 3HA

Author: Lisa Regan
Additional text: Ella Fern and Fiona Tulloch
Designer: Trudi Webb
Editors: Becca Clunes and Susie Rae
Design manager: Jessica Holliland
Editorial manager: Joe Harris

ISBN: 978-1-3988-1999-3
CH0010214NT
Supplier 29, Date 0622, PI 00000996

Printed in China

CHILDREN'S ENCYCLOPEDIA OF QUESTIONS AND ANSWERS

CONTENTS

Why is knowledge so amazing?

We know more today about ourselves, our planet, and the universe than we have ever known before. New innovations in electronics and computers shape our lives in all kinds of ways. We can explore far into space and dive to the deepest parts of the ocean. The boundaries of knowledge are limitless. So, what will you learn about inside the pages of this book?

Chapter 1: The Universe

Find out about the solar system, stars and galaxies, and the space that stretches beyond.

Chapter 2: The Earth

The third-closest planet to the Sun, and the only planet with oxygen and water, explore the beautiful blue ball that we call home.

Chapter 3: Animals

From fish to frogs and hammerheads to hummingbirds, there is so much to see in the natural world. Prepare to be awestruck and amazed!

Chapter 4: The Human Body

Read about the brilliant machine that is the human body, plus how modern medicine helps to protect us and heal us when we're sick.

Chapter 5: Science and Technology

Take a look at how far technology has brought us, and brush up on the science behind it all.

What is the universe?

The universe is everything we can see, feel, touch, measure, or detect. It includes the planets and stars, but also living things, dust clouds, light, and even time. The universe contains billions of galaxies. Each galaxy contains millions or billions of stars.

Formation

The universe was formed more than 13 billion years ago. It is believed that it began as a small ball of fire. This fireball grew larger and larger until one day it exploded to form the universe that we know.

Galaxies

Galaxies are made up of stars, gas, and dust, and come in different shapes and sizes. Scientists have divided them into three categories based on their shapes. These are spiral, elliptical (oval), and irregular (any other shape).

Stars

A star is a luminous ball of gas held together by gravity. Stars are usually found in groups called clusters. Some clusters are made of loosely packed stars, while other stars are packed tightly to form a dense cluster.

The Sun

The Sun is the largest object in the solar system. It is made up of huge amounts of hydrogen and helium. Nuclear reactions in its central region emit a large amount of energy that makes the Sun glow.

The stars and other elements in the universe seem still to be moving away from each other. The universe is expanding.

Scientists think that the early universe was a dense cluster of matter.

Planets

Planets are large masses of matter that orbit around a star. Our solar system consists of eight planets, including Jupiter (pictured). Jupiter is the largest planet orbiting our Sun. More than a thousand Earths could fit inside it!

Space exploration

The first person to travel in space was Yuri Gagarin on April 12, 1961. He orbited the Earth once on this historic flight, which lasted one hour and 48 minutes. Since then, humans have walked on the Moon, sent probes to Pluto and beyond, and can live in space for months at a time.

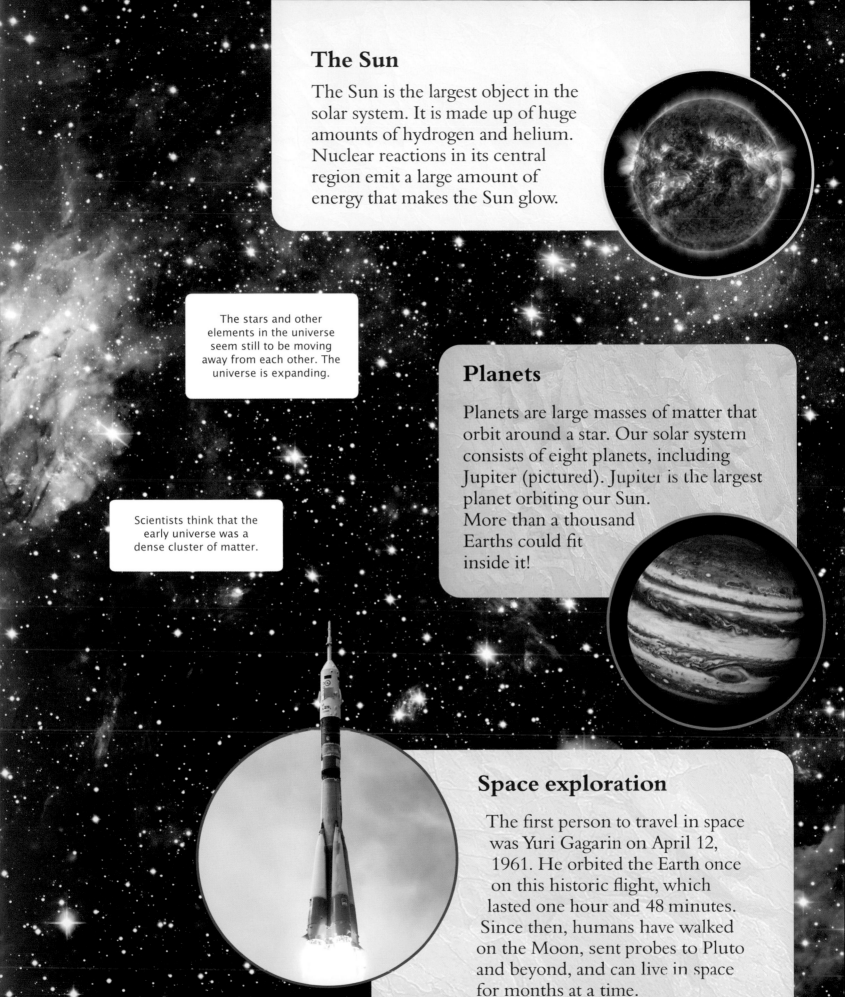

Galaxies

A galaxy is a group of millions or billions of stars, plus dust and gas, bound together by gravitational force. A galaxy can either be on its own or in a cluster.

What is the Big Bang theory?

This theory suggests that the universe as we know it today was created after a huge explosion. Georges Lemaître proposed the theory in 1927, and in 1929 Edwin Hubble expanded on his work.

How many galaxies are there?

We know of at least 100 billion. However, this number keeps growing as better telescopes are developed and we see more and more galaxies.

Which galaxy is Earth in?

Our solar system, including the Sun and the Earth, is in a galaxy called the Milky Way.

The Milky Way is part of a larger cluster known as the Local Group. Three of the 35 galaxies in the Local Group can be seen without a telescope. They are Andromeda and the Large and Small Magellanic Clouds.

IS IT TRUE THAT WE'RE GOING TO CRASH INTO ANOTHER GALAXY?

Sometimes, galaxies do crash, because of the force of gravity. But the stars in them are too far apart to cause any real damage. Our own galaxy is on a collision course with Andromeda. The collision will take place in about 4 billion years and the two will merge to form an elliptical galaxy.

DID YOU KNOW? It takes the Sun over 220 million years to orbit once around the middle of the Milky Way.

How big is the Milky Way?

It is huge. It takes the Sun about 250 million years to orbit once around the middle of the Milky Way.

How did the Milky Way get its name?

In ancient Greek and Roman myths, it was believed that the goddess Hera (Juno) spilt milk across the sky, leaving a white streak.

Stars

A star is a huge ball of gas and dust that gives out both heat and light. When the gases in the star burn out, it dies. A star can live for millions, even billions, of years depending on its size.

How many stars are there in a galaxy?

Each galaxy in the universe is made up of several billion stars.

What is a protostar?

Stars are born in clouds of dust and gases, mainly hydrogen. More and more gas is pulled together by gravity to form a cloud. After a while, the cloud begins to spin. This makes the gas atoms bump into each other at high speeds, creating a great deal of heat. As the cloud becomes hotter a nuclear reaction takes place inside, and the cloud begins to glow. This glowing cloud is called a protostar. It continues to contract until it becomes a star.

What is a supernova?

It is a vast explosion in which an entire star is destroyed. Afterward, extremely bright light is emitted for several days.

How long does a star live?

It glows for millions of years until the gases in its outer layer begin to cool, and the hydrogen in the inner core is slowly used up.

Supernovas mostly occur in distant galaxies. Because the stars are so far away, we may see a supernova explosion long after it takes place.

WHAT IS A CONSTELLATION?

Constellations are star patterns. They are made by drawing imaginary lines between the stars, to form familiar shapes. Astronomers have identified 88 constellations.

What is a white dwarf?

A small star usually shrinks to form a dense white dwarf, similar to the size of Earth.

Can we see white dwarf stars?

White dwarf stars are too dim to be detected without a telescope.

DID YOU KNOW? Supernovas are a billion times brighter than the Sun.

11

The Sun

The Sun is a medium-sized star that sits right at the heart of our solar system. Its energy travels through space and reaches us on Earth as heat and light.

How was the Sun created?

Before it was formed, the Sun, and the rest of the solar system, was a huge mass of hot gas and dust called a solar nebula. This nebula spun faster and faster until the clouds of gases, dust, and ice particles clumped together and exploded, forming the Sun.

What is the corona?

It is the glowing atmosphere of the Sun that extends far out into space. It is 200 times hotter than the Sun's surface.

How old is the Sun?

Our solar system was formed about 5 billion years ago, and the surface of the Sun is about 4.6 billion years old. It is younger and smaller than most stars in the universe.

Will the Sun ever disappear?

In about 5 billion years, when all the hydrogen in its core has been used up, the Sun will change into a red giant star. After that, the Sun will evolve into a white dwarf, before finally dying out.

A solar eclipse occurs when the Moon comes between the Sun and the Earth, blocking the Sun from view.

Does the Sun rotate?

Yes, it takes an average of about 26 days to rotate on its axis.

Sometimes, the Sun produces a huge amount of magnetic energy that sends out jets of gas called solar flares.

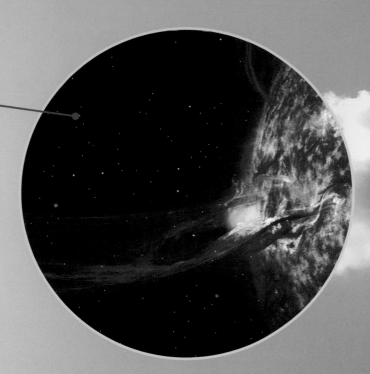

How far away is the Sun?

It is about 150 million km (93 million mi) away from the Earth.

HOW DO WE KNOW ABOUT THE SUN?

Several missions have been sent to study the Sun. The first detailed observations were made by NASA's Pioneer missions that were launched between 1959 and 1968. Probes such as SOHO and Parker are still out there collecting data.

DID YOU KNOW? Solar flares were observed for the first time in 1859.

Planets

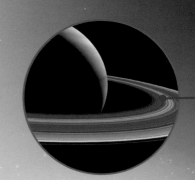

Our solar system consists of eight planets: Mercury, Venus, Earth, Mars, Jupiter, Saturn, Uranus, and Neptune. The first four are called the inner or rocky planets. The others are the outer planets, also known as gas giants.

How were the rocky planets formed?

After the gaseous cloud called the solar nebula collapsed in on itself due to the strength of its own gravity and formed the Sun, the dust and particles around it clumped together to form the planets. The heat of the Sun melted the ice and eventually these rocks grew larger to form four planets.

How did the gas giants form?

Some ice particles were too far away from the Sun to be melted. These ice pieces combined with gases to form the outer planets.

Some planets, such as Venus and Mars, can be seen from Earth at night.

How did the planets get their names?

All the planets are named after Roman gods and goddesses. Venus is named after the goddess of love. The surface features of Venus are also named after goddesses; for example, the planet has a deep canyon named Diana after the goddess of hunting.

Saturn is famous for the rings that surround it. Jupiter and Uranus also have rings.

Which planet is the hottest?

Although Mercury is closest to the Sun, Venus is even hotter, as carbon dioxide in its atmosphere traps the Sun's heat.

Why does the Earth look blue?

The Earth appears blue from outer space because over 70 percent of its surface is covered with water.

WHAT IS A MOON?

Also known as natural satellites, moons are objects that orbit planets. There are more than 180 moons in our solar system. Earth has just one moon, known by astronomers as Luna.

DID YOU KNOW? Mercury and Venus are the only planets in the solar system that have no moons.

15

Rocky planets

These four planets are made up of rocks and metals such as iron and nickel. They are smaller than the gas giants but are very heavy. Rocky planets rotate more slowly than the gas giants because of their weight.

What direction do the planets spin?

All the planets rotate from west to east on their axes (that's why, on Earth, the Sun rises in the east and sets in the west). There is an exception: Venus spins in the opposite direction.

Why is Mercury so cold at night?

The temperature changes dramatically because, unlike Earth, Mercury is not surrounded by a thick protective blanket of air (the atmosphere). This means that, even though the planet is closest to the Sun, the heat escapes at night. Daytime temperatures can reach 467°C (873°F) but drop to -183°C (-297°F) at night.

Why is a day longer than a year on Venus?

Venus goes around the Sun at a very high speed. It takes only about 225 days to complete one orbit. However, it spins much more slowly on its axis, taking about 243 days to complete a rotation. Therefore, days on Venus are longer than years.

There are many more volcanoes on Venus than there are on Earth.

Why is Mars called the Red Planet?

It glows red in the sky. Its surface is reddish–brown because of rust (iron oxide) in the ground.

DID YOU KNOW? A day on Mercury is equal to 176 Earth days!

WHY IS MERCURY'S SURFACE SO BUMPY?

Looked at closely, the surface can be seen to be pitted with huge craters. Any meteor that comes near Mercury falls on the surface and creates a crater, as there is no atmosphere to burn up the meteor.

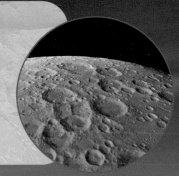

What is Mars like?

Its surface is divided into northern plains, flattened by lava flows, and southern highlands, marked by huge craters. Its atmosphere is 95 percent carbon dioxide.

Gas giants

These four planets are bigger than the inner planets, but lighter, as they are mainly made up of gases and ice particles. They spin extremely quickly. They do not have a hard surface, but Jupiter and Saturn do have a semi-liquid middle that is covered by a layer of liquid and gas.

Why do Saturn's rings shine?

They consist of dust particles and pieces of ice that can be quite large. The ice pieces reflect light, causing the rings to shine.

What is the Great Red Spot?

Jupiter is a stormy planet. The biggest storm area is called the Great Red Spot. It is so big that it can be seen from Earth through a telescope. Its winds rage at speeds of up to 640 km/h (400 mph).

The Voyager space probe was launched in 1977 and is still sending data to Earth. It has made flybys of Jupiter, Saturn, and Saturn's largest moon, Titan.

Who discovered Uranus?

It was the first planet to be seen through a telescope. It was discovered in 1781 by astronomer William Herschel. He initially reported it as a comet.

Uranus is unusual as it is the only planet that rotates from top to bottom as it orbits the Sun.

Why is Neptune blue?

Neptune contains methane. Sunlight is reflected by clouds under the methane layer. Only the blue portion of the reflected light passes through the methane layer, so the planet appears to be blue.

How strong are Neptune's winds?

Neptune is the windiest of the eight planets. Its winds reach speeds of about 2,000 km/h (1,200 mph), which is more than 10 times the speed of the strongest hurricane on Earth.

WHICH PLANET HAS THE MOST MOONS?

Jupiter has more known moons than any other planet, and we are still discovering new ones. Some do not even have names yet.

DID YOU KNOW? Saturn is so light that it would float if it were placed in water.

19

Moons

There are many moons in our solar system, which orbit planets, just like planets orbit the Sun. Earth has one moon, Mars has two small moons, while the gas giants have lots!

What is our Moon made of?

The Earth's Moon is made up of rocks, both solid and molten.

What is the dark side of the Moon?

We only see one side of the Moon because of the way it rotates. The side we see is called the near side, and the other side is the dark side. The first time people saw it was when astronauts orbited the Moon and took photographs.

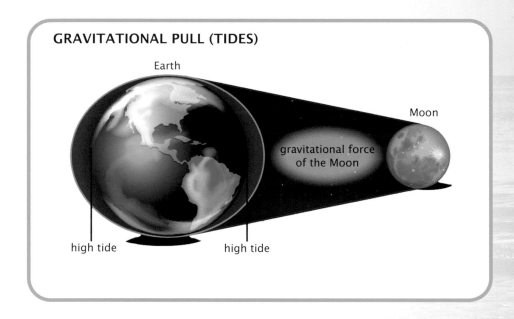

GRAVITATIONAL PULL (TIDES)

Earth

Moon

gravitational force of the Moon

high tide

high tide

The Moon's gravitational pull affects the Earth's oceans.

How does our Moon cause tides in our oceans?

Tides are caused by the gravitational force exerted by the Moon on our planet. This force causes the ocean to bulge out, making the tide rise. As the Earth is also pulled toward the Moon, the ocean on the side facing away from the Moon also bulges out.

Why can't we see the Moon during the day?

During the day, the bright light of the Sun blocks the soft glow of light reflected by the Moon.

What is a supermoon?

It is what astronomers call a perigean moon. That is, a full moon occurring near the time when the Moon is closer to the Earth, because the Moon's orbit is oval rather than circular.

HOW DOES OUR MOON GIVE OFF LIGHT?

It does not give off any light of its own. It simply reflects the sunlight that falls on it. As the Moon orbits Earth, we see only a part of it that is lit up by the Sun.

DID YOU KNOW? Tides are higher in the tropics due to the bulge of the equator.

Dwarf planets

Not everything in a Solar System is a planet. A dwarf planet is categorized by the International Astronomical Union (IAU) as a celestial body that has enough mass to form a round shape, orbits the Sun, is not a moon, and has not cleared the area around its orbit. The best-known dwarf planet is Pluto.

How is a dwarf planet different?

According to the IAU's definition, a planet is a space object that orbits the Sun and has a nearly round shape. Its gravity must be strong enough to clear all other space objects (except satellites) out of its orbit. Dwarf planets are not big enough for their gravitational fields to do this.

What changed with Pluto?

Pluto was once classed as the ninth planet in our solar system. But in 2006, it was officially reclassified as a dwarf planet, because it is so small and its gravitational field is not as strong as that of the major planets.

Why aren't dwarf planets just satellites?

Satellites orbit a planet, not the Sun.

How many dwarf planets are there?

The IAU lists five: Pluto, Ceres, Eris, Makemake, and Haumea. The first two have been known for about a hundred years, but the other three were only discovered at the start of the twenty-first century.

Ceres was the first dwarf planet to be visited by a spacecraft, in January 2015.

Until 2006, Ceres was classified as the largest asteroid.

Have any space probes visited Pluto?

New Horizons, launched in 2006, made it all the way to Pluto and beyond in 2015. It sent back important images of Pluto and Charon.

HOW DO DWARF PLANETS GET THEIR NAMES?

The dwarf planets are named after characters from mythology. Pluto is the Roman god of the underworld, Ceres is the Roman god of grain, and Eris, Makemake, and Haumea are the Greek, Rapa Nui, and Hawaiian gods of fertility.

Does Pluto have any moons?

Pluto has five moons. One of them, Charon, is almost half the size of Pluto itself.

DID YOU KNOW? Eris is the largest of all the dwarf planets.

23

Comets and asteroids

Together with the Sun, the planets, and their moons, several other objects are also part of the solar system. These are asteroids, comets, or meteors, and they are made up of small pieces of rock, metal, and ice.

What are asteroids?

When the solar system was formed, some fragments of rock were left spinning in space. These huge space rocks that orbit the Sun are called asteroids. Like some planets, asteroids are made of metals such as iron, and have moons. Some of them are called minor planets.

What is a comet?

A comet is made of ice and other material. As it nears the Sun, these materials heat up. Solar wind and pressure from the Sun's radiation push them outward to form a tail that always points away from the Sun.

Most of the asteroids in our solar system are in a belt between the orbits of Mars and Jupiter.

Are asteroids dangerous?

An asteroid can be thrown off its orbit by the gravity of a planet or another asteroid. It often strikes the surface of other planets or moons. Some scientists think that an asteroid struck Earth 66 million years ago, wiping out the dinosaurs.

Do meteors ever fall to Earth?

Sometimes, small fragments, called meteorites, crash onto the surface. Some are so big that they make craters where they fall.

How big can the craters be?

This one is in Australia and is the second largest in the world. It is called Wolfe Creek and measures roughly 880 m (2,890 ft) across.

Sometimes, lots of meteoroids can be seen at once, in a meteor shower.

DID YOU KNOW? Sungrazers are comets that crash into, or get very close to, the Sun.

25

Humans in space

Ever since ancient times, humans have wanted to know more about the skies above them. They invented stories to explain the presence of the stars, Moon, and Sun. Today's advanced technology helps us expand our knowledge about the world beyond our planet.

Spacecraft such as the SpaceX Dragon are used to carry passengers and cargo to the ISS.

How do we get into space?

All objects, even planes, are glued to the surface of the Earth by gravity. If you want to escape this unseen force, you have to travel at a speed of at least 40,000 km/h (25,000 mph). Space rockets burn a mixture of liquid hydrogen and liquid oxygen to push them into orbit.

Why is there no gravity in space?

All objects in space exert some gravitational force on each other. However, the force exerted by some objects, like the Moon, is much less than that of the Earth. When humans are in space they float around, because there is not enough gravity to keep their feet on the ground.

People on board the International Space Station (ISS) experience weightlessness. They have to keep their tools strapped to their body so they don't float away.

Is it possible to live in space?

Yes! Astronauts spend months at a time living on the ISS.

WHAT DO ASTRONAUTS DO ON THE ISS?

They spend much of their time doing research. They also exercise a lot. This sounds tiring and like hard work (and it is!), but they do get some time when they can read, or simply enjoy the spectacular view out of the ISS window!

Does the ISS move?

The ISS is permanently orbiting Earth, cruising at 27,700 km/h (17,200 mph) to stay in position.

The ISS completes one trip around the Earth every 92 minutes. Astronauts on board see 15 or 16 sunrises and sunsets every day.

DID YOU KNOW? The ISS is the ninth space station to have crew living on board.

27

What is Earth like?

The Earth is the third closest planet to the Sun, and the fifth largest, behind Jupiter, Saturn, Uranus, and Neptune. Studies of its rocks tell us that it is around 4.5 billion years old.

Is Earth like any other planets in our solar system?

Venus is closest to Earth because of its position and also in terms of its size, composition, and gravity. It is so similar to Earth that it is often considered to be its twin. However, Venus is very different. Its atmosphere is a lot thicker than Earth's and is mainly carbon dioxide, making Venus much, much hotter.

Is the Earth a perfect sphere?

No—it is more like a squished ball that bulges out at the equator.

The Earth is made of different layers, with a thin, rocky crust on the outside and a core in the middle made from nickel and iron.

How does Earth support life?

It has two things that living things need to survive: oxygen and water. It is also the right distance from the Sun for the temperature to be comfortable for living creatures.

WHAT CAUSES DAY AND NIGHT?

The Earth turning on its axis is responsible for day and night. At any time, half the Earth faces the Sun, where it is day, and half faces away, where it is night.

How fast does Earth travel around the Sun?

Earth moves at around 30 km (18.6 mi) per second! It takes one year, or just over 365 days, for it to complete one full orbit.

Where do most people live?

There are more than 7 billion people on Earth, but they aren't distributed evenly across the land. Over half of the global population lives in urban areas (towns and cities).

Earth's year is split into seasons, defined by distinct weather. The seasons are caused by the tilt in the Earth's axis.

DID YOU KNOW? The first images of Earth from space were taken by German rockets in 1947.

What makes Earth unique?

Earth is a rocky planet orbiting the Sun. Its atmosphere protects us from the Sun's harmful rays, provides the air that we breathe and that plants need to grow, and keeps the Earth at the right temperature for living things to survive. Earth has huge amounts of water, which is also necessary for life. Sometimes, there are natural disasters.

Continents

Geographers divide the Earth's land into large areas called continents. These are landmasses that are thicker than the surrounding areas of the Earth's crust. They roughly correspond to the tectonic plates that move slowly on top of the liquid layers underneath.

Weather and climate

Clouds, rain, and snow form in the troposphere, the layer of the atmosphere closest to the Earth's surface. Sometimes, the weather is kind to us, providing sun and rain for crops to grow. Sometimes, extreme weather causes chaos.

Landforms

The movement of Earth's crust creates landforms such as mountains and valleys. They come in a variety of shapes, eroded through the centuries or carved out over millions of years. Water is present not only in the vast oceans, but also inland, in the form of streams, rivers, and lakes.

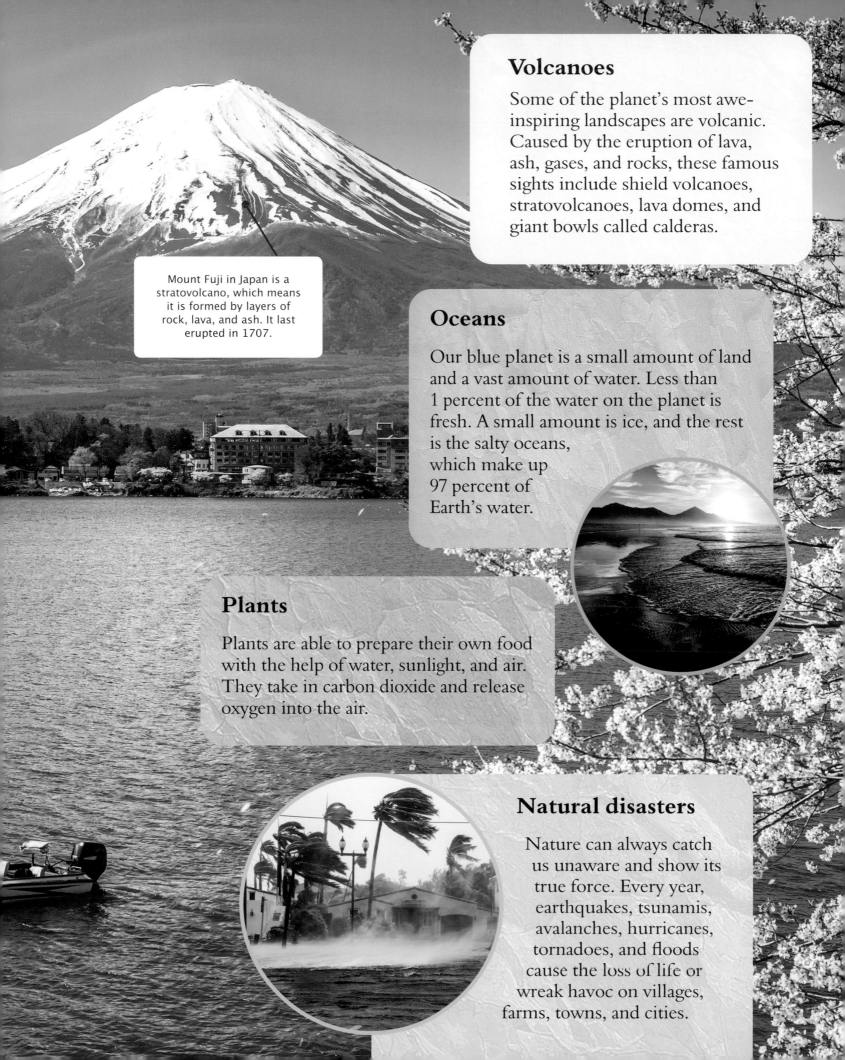

Volcanoes

Some of the planet's most awe-inspiring landscapes are volcanic. Caused by the eruption of lava, ash, gases, and rocks, these famous sights include shield volcanoes, stratovolcanoes, lava domes, and giant bowls called calderas.

Mount Fuji in Japan is a stratovolcano, which means it is formed by layers of rock, lava, and ash. It last erupted in 1707.

Oceans

Our blue planet is a small amount of land and a vast amount of water. Less than 1 percent of the water on the planet is fresh. A small amount is ice, and the rest is the salty oceans, which make up 97 percent of Earth's water.

Plants

Plants are able to prepare their own food with the help of water, sunlight, and air. They take in carbon dioxide and release oxygen into the air.

Natural disasters

Nature can always catch us unaware and show its true force. Every year, earthquakes, tsunamis, avalanches, hurricanes, tornadoes, and floods cause the loss of life or wreak havoc on villages, farms, towns, and cities.

Atmosphere

The protective blanket of air that covers the Earth is called the atmosphere. It not only prevents too much heat from entering the planet, but also protects us from asteroids and meteors. Earth's gravity helps hold the atmosphere in place.

Which gases make up our atmosphere?

Earth's atmosphere is composed mainly of nitrogen (around 78 percent) and oxygen (21 percent). The rest is carbon dioxide, water, and trace gases such as neon and helium.

Global warming is leading to the melting of glaciers and polar ice caps.

How many layers does the Earth's atmosphere have?

It is composed of several layers, which include the troposphere and the stratosphere. Each layer is divided according to the temperature and density of air within it.

What are greenhouse gases?

Gases such as carbon dioxide and CFCs in the atmosphere trap heat from the Sun. They are useful, but humans are adding more of them, which is leading to global warming.

How does the stratosphere help us?

The stratosphere is the layer just above the troposphere. It extends upward from the troposphere to about 50 km (31 mi) above the Earth's surface. Compared to the troposphere, which is full of moisture, the stratosphere is dry. The stratosphere contains the ozone layer. Ozone absorbs harmful ultraviolet rays from the Sun.

How does pollution affect the atmosphere?

Pollution from factories and vehicles is creating a dangerous hole in the protective ozone layer above the Earth, and increasing the Earth's temperature.

WHAT HAPPENS IN THE TROPOSPHERE?

The troposphere is the layer closest to Earth's surface, and it is here that weather is created. Air in the troposphere rises and falls, helping to form clouds, rain, and snow. This layer stretches about 8–14 km (5–9 mi) above sea level.

Chopping down forests is dangerously raising the level of greenhouse gases in the atmosphere. Trees absorb carbon dioxide, so if you cut them down, they can't do this.

DID YOU KNOW? Large volcanic eruptions also affect the Earth's atmosphere.

33

Weather and climate

The Earth not only orbits the Sun, but it also rotates on its own axis as it does so. The Earth's axis is tilted, meaning that neither of the poles faces the Sun directly. This tilted axis is responsible for weather and different climates.

The wind moves to the right in the northern hemisphere and the left in the southern. This "Coriolis effect" is mainly responsible for hurricanes.

How is weather different from climate?

Sunlight falls at varying angles onto the Earth's surface, heating up each of its regions differently. The difference in temperature eventually leads to different types of weather. A climate is when particular weather conditions continue in a place for an extended period of time.

What factors influence the weather?

Temperature, rainfall, wind, cloud, and atmospheric pressure are the main factors. Other factors, such as the ocean currents caused by the Earth's rotation, also have an effect.

Low pressure usually means stormy weather and rain. High pressure usually brings lots of sun and not much wind.

What causes the wind?

Wind is caused by the unequal heating of the Earth's surface. When the air above a certain region becomes warm and light, it rises and the heavier cool air sweeps across from another area to take its place.

What causes a thunderstorm?

These storms occur when there is warm air underneath a body of much colder air. They are most common where the weather is hot and humid.

What is lightning?

It is a series of sudden electrical discharges. The discharges cause flashes of light and rumbling sound waves.

HOW ARE CLOUDS FORMED?

The Sun's heat causes water in the oceans, rivers, and lakes to evaporate. This warm air rises and cools, and condenses back into water droplets. These form clouds and as the water droplets grow larger in size, they fall as rain.

DID YOU KNOW? About 2,000 thunderstorms occur on Earth every minute!

35

Continents

The surface of the Earth is divided into tectonic plates—massive slabs of rock on which all the land on the planet sits. The gradual movement of these plates is responsible for features like mountains and valleys, and ocean trenches and ridges.

Which is the largest continent?

Asia is the largest, covering nearly 30 percent of Earth's total landmass. It includes some of the world's most populated countries, such as China and India.

Oceans cover more than double the area of the planet compared to all the continents put together.

How big is Africa?

It is the second largest continent on the planet. It is home to 54 countries: Sudan is the largest and the Seychelles islands are the smallest.

Australia has a very low population density of only three people per sq km (eight per sq mi). There are far more sheep there than people!

Which continent has the fewest countries?

North America is the world's third largest continent but is only made up of three countries: Canada, the USA, and Mexico.

Is Antarctica a continent?

Yes, it is a landmass that is almost completely covered in ice.

Are any continents joined together?

Europe and Asia actually sit together on one plate and are a single, huge piece of land. Culturally and geographically, though, they count as separate continents.

What is Antarctica like?

It is the fifth largest continent and is nearly twice the size of Australia. It is the world's driest, windiest, least populated, and coldest continent.

HOW BIG IS SOUTH AMERICA?

It is the fourth largest continent but home to only 12 countries. It is also the location of the longest mountain range in the world, the Andes.

DID YOU KNOW? The Arctic is mostly ocean and sea ice, so does not count as a continent.

37

Mountains, valleys, and caves

Mountains are formed when two of the continental plates that make up Earth's crust collide. The force caused by the collision pushes both plates upward, creating a mountain. Valleys and caves are also natural features created by erosion and the movement of the Earth's crust.

What is the difference between a mountain and a plateau?

Like a mountain, a plateau is higher than its surrounding area. However, plateaus have a flat top, while mountains have peaks.

What is a valley?

It is a low-lying area of land that is usually found at the foot of mountains or hills. They are commonly formed by the erosion of land from running water. As a river flows downhill, it cuts through the land, usually forming a V-shaped valley.

A deep valley with cliffs on both sides is called a canyon. Sometimes, a large river might run through it.

HOW ARE CAVES FORMED?

Most are formed by rainwater that seeps into tiny cracks in the rocks. The rainwater contains chemicals that slowly dissolve the rock.

Are there different types of valley?

Yes. Valleys formed by glaciers rather than rivers tend to be U-shaped because they are worn away across the glacier's full width by rocks carried in the ice.

How do high altitudes affect people?

At very high altitudes, oxygen levels are so low that it becomes difficult to breathe without an oxygen tank and mask.

Sea caves are formed by waves that wear away the rocks at the base of a cliff. Some can only be seen at low tide.

Can we live on mountains?

It isn't easy to live on high mountains. The weather is very cold and not suitable for farming.

DID YOU KNOW? The Himalayan mountains are getting taller every year!

39

Rivers, lakes, and streams

Rivers, lakes, and streams are natural bodies of water found across the world. Rainwater or melting snow flows downhill, forming streams. Several streams join together to form a river. The water keeps flowing until it reaches the sea, though a few rivers hit very dry desert land and dry up.

Which is the longest river?

The Nile is the longest river on Earth. It flows for 6,695 km (4,184 mi) in northeastern Africa.

How do rivers flood?

Rivers often overflow their banks and flood the land around them. It can happen when there has been a lot of rain or melted snow. Floods can damage crops and destroy houses.

How are lakes formed?

Sometimes, rainwater collects in big hollows in the ground. These hollows can be formed by the movement of Earth's plates, or by moving glaciers. Lakes are also formed by landslides that leave huge depressions in the ground.

The Amazon river in South America is the world's largest river, carrying around one fifth of all the world's river water.

Lake Baikal in Russia is the world's deepest lake. It has been around for almost 30 million years.

What is a waterfall?

Sometimes, the surface over which a river flows drops suddenly. Then the water flows over to form a waterfall.

DID YOU KNOW? The place where a river meets the ocean is called the river mouth.

CAN LAKES BE SALTY?

Most lakes contain freshwater but in places containing high levels of salt, the lake can be salty. If no rivers flow out of the lake, the water evaporates, leaving the salt behind.

Are there different types of waterfall?

A cascade waterfall flows down a series of natural rock steps. There are no steps in a free–falling waterfall. In a fan waterfall, the water spreads out as it falls.

Oceans

Oceans occupy around 70 percent of the Earth's surface. The surface under the oceans is called the ocean floor. Like land, the ocean floor also has natural features such as plains, valleys, and mountains.

How many oceans are there?

There is only one vast body of water but it is divided into five named geographical areas. These are the Atlantic, Pacific, Indian, Arctic, and Southern oceans.

Until 2000, the Southern Ocean was considered to be part of the other main oceans. Now it is separate.

What is the ocean floor like?

The edges of islands and continents gently slope into the surrounding water to form an area called a continental shelf. This is higher than the rest of the ocean floor. It drops away steeply toward the deep canyons of the ocean.

What creates ocean currents?

An ocean current is a mass of water that keeps moving in one direction. Surface currents are caused by wind and the Earth's rotation. Underwater currents are the result of differences in temperature and salt content of the water.

How do islands appear?

Some of the mountains on the ocean floor are tall enough for their peaks to rise above the surface and form islands.

HOW ARE WAVES DIFFERENT FROM TIDES?

Waves are formed when winds blow over the surface of the ocean, while tides are the regular rise and fall of the ocean's surface caused by gravitational pull.

How are volcanic islands formed?

They are created by volcanoes under the sea. As magma keeps oozing out of a volcano, it can collect, causing the volcano to grow and rise above the ocean surface as an island.

Marine life thrives in the shallower waters of a continental shelf.

DID YOU KNOW? The Pacific Ocean is the world's largest and deepest ocean.

43

Plants

Plants are one of the biggest groups of living things and are unique to Earth. There are around 350,000 species, which include trees, shrubs, vines, ferns, grasses, mosses, and lichen. Green plants can produce their own food using water and nutrients from the soil and sunlight.

What do plants need to grow?

Different plants have different needs, but all plants need food. Most need soil, air, water, and sunlight to produce food. Some grow in the desert and are used to little or no water. Others can grow in water and need little soil.

Why do plants have roots?

Roots hold down a plant and keep it steady. With most plants, the roots grow first. They absorb water and minerals from the soil and transport them up so the plant can produce food. Some plants have aerial roots (roots in the air) growing from the branches.

Why do plants grow flowers and fruit?

They do it to reproduce. The flowers contain pollen, which are carried by insects or the wind to other plants for reproduction. The fruit contains seeds of new plants, which are carried by animals, wind, or water to other places where a new plant can grow.

A fern has neither flowers nor seeds. They grow from spores on the leaves that are scattered by the wind.

What are mangroves?

Mangroves are tropical plants that grow near the coast and are partly covered by sea water when the tide flows in.

WHAT IS A CARNIVOROUS PLANT?

Some plants, like the venus flytrap, butterwort, and corkscrew plants, get their nutrients from eating insects. The pitcher plant has a deep tube filled with a liquid that attracts insects. The walls are built so that insects can climb down but not climb up again. Slowly, they drown, and are digested by the plant.

Do mangroves have special roots?

They have stilt roots to prop them up. These roots can breathe through special pores.

DID YOU KNOW? Some plants contain deadly poisons to stop them from being eaten.

45

Volcanoes

A volcano is a mountain through which molten rock and gases erupt from the Earth's crust. Volcanoes are named after the Roman god of fire, Vulcan.

How are volcanoes formed?

They form when tectonic plates collide with each other. The heavier plate is usually forced down below the lighter one, where part of it is melted by the heat of the crash. The melting plate forms magma (molten rock) that collects below the surface in magma chambers. As the amount increases, the pressure rises and creates a volcano.

How often do volcanoes erupt?

It varies. Some erupt often, and are called active volcanoes. Intermittent volcanoes erupt at regular intervals. Dormant volcanoes have been inactive for a long time. They are dangerous as they can erupt without warning. Extinct volcanoes have not erupted for thousands of years.

A geyser is a jet of hot water that erupts. Water trickles into the hot molten rock beneath the Earth's crust, heats up, and then spurts out.

What comes out of a volcano?

It isn't just lava that comes out of a volcano. Pieces of rock and ash also erupt. These volcanic materials are called pyroclasts.

When the pressure inside a volcano gets too high, the whole magma chamber explodes, ejecting the magma.

What is a stratovolcano?

It is a steep volcano shaped like a cone. They are the most dangerous volcanoes on Earth.

WHAT IS LAVA?

Magma that erupts to the surface is called lava. It can be thick and quite slow-moving, or thin and fast.

DID YOU KNOW? A volcano in Iceland erupted in 2021 after 800 years of inactivity.

47

Earthquakes and tsunamis

The Earth's crust sits on top of a hot, liquid middle. When the crust's tectonic plates move around, they sometimes collide and cause earthquakes. If these earthquakes occur under the ocean, they can cause tsunamis.

Where do earthquakes happen?

They usually occur along a region called a fault, where broken rocks under the Earth's surface rub against each other and cause tremors. Faults are marked by cracks on the surface. Most are near the edges of plates, but some are found far from these boundaries.

Are all earthquakes dangerous?

Some are so small that they are hardly felt. But others are so massive that they cause the ground to shake violently, destroying houses and killing people.

An earthquake can shake the ground enough to set off a deadly avalanche. It may cause more damage than the original earthquake.

What is a tsunami like?

They are giant, destructive waves that move at great speeds and can travel great distances across the ocean. In deep water, the waves are not very high. They gain strength and height as they approach the land. The huge waves break onto the shore with a great deal of force.

The 2011 tsunami in Japan destroyed more than 123,000 houses and damaged many more.

DID YOU KNOW? Tsunamis can be about 30 m (98 ft) high.

**How destructive
are earthquakes?**

A strong quake can
topple buildings and
bridges, trapping people
underneath. Earthquakes
can start fires if gas pipes
or electrical wires break.

**How are earthquakes
measured?**

They are measured
on the Richter scale.
It uses numbers from
1 to 10 to measure
the intensity of the
earthquake.

Wild weather

Sometimes, we experience severe weather that causes a great deal of damage to both life and property. Blizzards, thunderstorms, hurricanes, tornadoes, and heatwaves can all be problematic or extremely destructive.

What is a hurricane?

A hurricane is a large, violent storm that forms over the ocean near the equator. These storms are accompanied by winds that travel over 100 km/h (60 mph). Hurricanes usually occur between June and November.

How does a hurricane form?

When the air above the sea is heated it rises, creating an area of low pressure. Cooler wind moves in to take the place of the warm air. The Earth's rotation causes the rising hot air to twist and form a cylinder. As the warm air rises higher, it cools down and finally becomes a hurricane. Meanwhile, the cooler air at the bottom also becomes warm, adding more energy to the storm.

What is the eye of the hurricane?

The middle of the hurricane is called the "eye." It is an area of clear skies, light winds, and no rain. It is surrounded by a wall of heavy rain and strong winds.

Visibility is reduced during a blizzard, sometimes to "white out" conditions, which make travel impossible.

What is a tornado?

It is a black, funnel-shaped storm that is highly destructive. They start as rotating thunderstorms, called supercells.

DID YOU KNOW? Hurricanes are graded into categories, with one as the weakest and five as the strongest.

WHAT IS A WATERSPOUT?

When a tornado passes over water, it sucks the water up into a tall spinning column. Waterspouts are weaker than land tornadoes but still dangerous to boats.

Where do tornadoes form?

These storms usually form where cold polar winds mix with warm, moist tropical winds. They are common in the central USA in an area known as Tornado Alley.

The wind in a tornado spins so fast that it sucks objects into it like a vacuum cleaner. Flying debris is very dangerous.

What animals live on our planet?

There are millions of species of animals on Earth. Animals are living things that have to find food and can usually move around to do so. Some animals have a backbone, and are classed as vertebrates. There arc many more invertebrates (animals without a backbone)—well over 90 percent of creatures on the planet are invertebrates.

Mammals

This group of warm-blooded vertebrates have certain things in common, but can appear very different. In this chapter, we take a closer look at lots of types, from apes and wolves to whales and elephants.

Reptiles

The animals in this category have a backbone, scaly skin, and either four legs or none at all. Most lay eggs but some give birth to live young. They are cold-blooded, so can't keep warm without help.

Insects

One of the most common types of invertebrates is insects. They have a body with a hard outer casing and three parts. Adult insects have six legs and wings.

Birds

These two-legged vertebrates have feathers and wings, although not all of them can fly. They have a horn-like beak, or bill, instead of a mouth with teeth. Their young hatch from eggs.

Amphibians

An amphibious creature is happy on land or in water. The adults usually lay their eggs in or near water. The hatchlings breathe underwater with gills, but develop lungs as they get older. Like reptiles, they are cold-blooded and so take on the temperature of their surroundings.

Fish

Fish are vertebrates that spend their whole lives in water, breathing through gills. They have no legs. They are covered in scales for protection and have fins to help them swim.

Birds

Birds live in various habitats and spend different amounts of time on land or in the air. Many survive by eating invertebrates and seeds, but others eat bigger creatures, such as fish, mammals, and other birds.

What are birds of prey?

Also called raptors, birds of prey are meat-eating birds that use their claws and beak to hunt. They include vultures, hawks, eagles, kites, falcons, harriers, buzzards, secretary birds, and owls.

How sharp are their senses?

A raptor's sharp ears can hear prey moving and tell how far away it is. They have larger eyes than most other birds, and excellent vision.

How can you identify a raptor?

Raptors like the American bald eagle have a sharp, curved beak and strong feet with powerful claws (talons).

An owl's wings have soft, round edges for flying slowly and silently.

DID YOU KNOW? Seabirds have glands on their face that get rid of the excess salt they take in from the seawater.

Songbirds lay their first clutch of eggs when they are less than a year old. The eggs often hatch after just 10 days.

Can all birds sing?

No. Those that can are called songbirds, and have specially developed vocal cords (syringes), which they use to produce songs. Some, like the wood thrush, can control both syringes separately and sing two songs at the same time. Songbirds have a special section in their brain that helps them to learn their songs.

What are waterfowl?

This family includes ducks, swans, and geese. They have webbed feet to help them paddle, and flat bills. Their feathers have a coating of oil that works like waterproofing.

WHERE DO SONGBIRDS LIVE?

Most of them live in trees and often feed on fruit, berries, and insects. Eight out of every 10 perching birds are songbirds, including the blue jay (pictured) and all other members of the crow family.

Flightless birds

Not all birds can fly. Some have wings that are too short and weak to take to the air. Most flightless birds are found on small islands. New Zealand has the largest number, from kiwis and penguins to the kakapo, the world's only flightless parrot.

Why can't they fly?

All flying birds have a keel, or breastbone, to which powerful flight muscles are attached. In flightless birds, this keel is either very small or completely absent. This makes their wings too weak to fly.

Which is the smallest flightless bird?

The Inaccessible Island rail, of the South Atlantic. It is no more than 17 cm (7 in) long and weighs less than 30 g (1 oz)—about the same as a pencil.

The kakapo is nocturnal. It cannot fly but it can climb very well.

The emu is Australia's tallest bird. Adults have shaggy brown feathers but the chicks are striped.

WHICH ARE THE MOST COMMON FLIGHTLESS BIRDS?

Penguins are the most common. They are found in many different places, nearly all in the southern hemisphere. Some have a thick layer of blubber (fat) that protects them from freezing temperatures, allowing them to live as far south as Antarctica.

Which flightless bird is the biggest?

The ostrich is the largest flightless bird, and the biggest of all living birds.

What is a kiwi bird?

The national symbol of New Zealand, the kiwi is a small, shy, nocturnal bird. It has a keen sense of smell, with nostrils on the end of its long beak. It pushes its beak into the ground in search of food.

How do they stay safe?

An ostrich can outrun most predators and can deliver a fatal kick with its clawed feet.

DID YOU KNOW? A penguin's wings act as flippers underwater, pushing them along at speed.

57

Fish

Fish were some of the earliest creatures to inhabit the Earth. They appeared about 500 to 475 million years ago. The first fish were jawless and finless, like the lamprey and hagfish that still exist today.

Do fish have skeletons?

Most fish have a bony skeleton inside. One group has a skeleton made of cartilage instead of bone (see page 60). Bony fish are divided into two groups: lobe-finned fish (which includes lungfish) and ray-finned fish (which include well-known fish such as herring, tuna, salmon, sunfish, and flatfish).

Are all fish the same shape?

Many fish have the same body shape: slim and streamlined to glide through the water. Others are shorter and more rounded. Some, like eels, are very long and slender. Others, like flatfish, have a body like a dinner plate so they can hide on the ocean floor or river bed.

Can fish fly?

Some have fins that are large enough to propel them out of the water, so they look like they are flying. Flying fish can cover 30–50 m (98–164 ft) in one glide. Hatchetfish, which live in the Amazon, have wing-like pectoral fins which they beat as they fly short distances.

The male stickleback builds a nest of algae and plants for its eggs. It holds the nest together with a sticky substance from its body.

Most fish live either in freshwater (such as rivers and lakes) or in saltwater, but not in both.

Do fish go to sleep?

Members of the parrotfish family, like this one, sleep at night. But most other fish swim slowly when they are resting.

DID YOU KNOW? Some fish, like salmon, live in the sea but move into rivers to breed.

What are the fins called?

A fish usually has pectoral, dorsal, and caudal (tail) fins that help it to swim and stop it from rolling over.

HOW DO FISH REPRODUCE?

Most fish lay eggs and then swim away, leaving their eggs and hatchlings unprotected. However, the female seahorse (a type of fish, despite its unusual appearance!) lays her eggs in the male's pouch. He carries them until they hatch.

Sharks and rays

Sharks and rays are the oldest fish on Earth. They were here even before the dinosaurs. These fish have cartilage or tough tissue instead of bones. They breathe through gill slits and have very distinctive skin and jaws.

What is shark skin like?

Sharks don't have scales like bony fish. Instead, their skin is covered with small tooth-shaped growths called denticles. These give the fish a rough, sandpapery texture.

What is a ray?

Rays belong to the same family as sharks but have a flat, kite-like body that helps them to glide through the ocean. There are thousands of species of rays, including eagle rays, manta rays, and stingrays.

How big are sharks?

The biggest is enormous and the smallest is tiny! The pygmy ribbontail catshark grows to just 24 cm (9.5 in) long. The largest is the whale shark, which reaches 15 m (50 ft) but eats tiny sea creatures.

How do sharks hunt?

Not all sharks are fierce killers. However, those that hunt have a strong sense of smell and a good sense of hearing.

Is this a whale or a shark?

Despite its name, a whale shark is a shark, not a whale. It is a cartilaginous fish like all sharks and rays.

The upper part of a thresher shark's tail fin is exceptionally long.

HOW MANY TEETH DOES A SHARK HAVE?

Sharks may have up to 3,000 teeth at one time. Various species of sharks have teeth of different shapes and sizes. This great white shark has sharp, wide, wedge-shaped and serrated teeth that allow it to catch and tear its prey.

How did the whale shark get its name?

It is named because of its enormous size —like that of whales. The whale shark is the world's biggest shark, and so is also the biggest fish.

Sharks have extra senses to detect electrical fields created by their prey.

DID YOU KNOW? The great white shark can live up to one hundred years.

61

Reptiles

The word reptile means "to creep." Most reptiles are covered with scales or plates to keep their skin moist. They breathe through lungs. Certain lizards and snakes give birth to live young, but most reptiles build nests and lay eggs in them.

The fierce Komodo dragon is the biggest lizard in the world.

How many eggs do reptiles lay?

Some tortoises lay only one egg in a season. Turtles lay about 150 eggs several times per season. Snakes can lay anything from three to 100 eggs, while crocodiles lay 20–90 eggs at a time.

Why do turtles have a shell?

A turtle's upper and lower shell is for protection. It is part of the turtle's body, and is made up of bones, skin, and keratin. Sea turtles cannot pull their head back into their shell like their land-based relatives can.

What is a snake's skin like?

It is smooth and silky to touch, but not slimy. A snake's skin is made up of protective scales. It even has transparent scales to protect its eyes. As a snake grows, it sheds its skin. The old skin peels off like a sock, beginning at the mouth.

What is the shell like?

The upper shell is called the carapace and is usually dome-shaped. The flat lower shell is called the plastron.

DID YOU KNOW? Emerald tree boas are born red or orange but turn green as they grow.

A snake "hears" with an inner ear that senses vibrations in the ground.

How do turtles breathe?

Turtles breathe using lungs but only need to come to the surface to breathe every now and then.

ARE REPTILES VENOMOUS?

They can be! Some lizards have a poisonous bite, such as the gila monster and beaded lizard. Many snakes are venomous, including mambas, cobras (pictured), vipers, and sea snakes.

More reptiles

Crocodilians, a group that includes alligators and caimans as well as crocodiles, lived up to 100 million years ago in the Cretaceous Period —when dinosaurs (which were also reptiles) roamed the Earth!

How did reptiles first appear?

About 300 million years ago, amphibians adapted to their environment and evolved into reptiles. They developed a better way of breathing than amphibians and as a result, they could take in more air. These primitive reptiles evolved into dinosaurs about 210 million years ago.

What did dinosaurs eat?

Despite their reputation, about 65 percent of the dinosaurs were plant-eaters, not aggressive carnivores. They lived at the time when the first flowering plants were developing, but mostly ate fern-like plants.

Is that a crocodile or an alligator?

The two look similar, but are in fact very different. Alligators only live in the wild in the USA and parts of China. Their range hardly crosses over with any crocodiles. Visually, a crocodile's snout and teeth help to tell it apart from an alligator.

The caiman is the main crocodilian found in Central and South America, especially in the Amazon rain forests.

An alligator has a broad, U–shaped snout. The snout of a crocodile is usually a narrower V–shape.

ARE CROCODILIANS GOOD PARENTS?

Crocodilian mothers build nests to lay their eggs and are extremely protective. Unlike other reptiles, they don't abandon their eggs. Instead, the mother stays close to keep predators away. After hatching, she takes her young for a swim, often carrying them in her mouth. The mother looks after her babies for about a year.

How do they see?

A crocodilian's eyes are on top of their head so they can still see when their body is submerged.

How do the teeth help to identify what it is?

A crocodile's upper and lower teeth are visible even when its mouth is closed.

DID YOU KNOW? Crocodilians usually swallow their prey whole or tear off huge chunks. They cannot chew.

Amphibians

There are around 6,000 species of amphibian and most of them begin their life in water. An amphibian's skin is thin and moist and helps it to breathe. They need to live in damp places.

Lots of other animals eat frogs' eggs, so frogs lay enough to be sure that some survive.

How do amphibians give birth?

Most amphibians are born in water, where the eggs are laid. Although some frogs, toads, and caecilians give birth to live young that look like adults, most frogs lay eggs in a blob of jelly. Most toads lay eggs in long strips of gel.

What changes happen as they grow?

What are their eyes like?

Frogs and toads have bulging eyes covered by a transparent piece of skin to keep their eyes moist.

All amphibians are born from an egg and grow into a tadpole. As the tadpole grows, its eyes grow eyelids and it learns to see in and out of water. Tadpoles lose their tail before they move onto land and become adults.

Why are they important?

Frogs and toads help to keep insects under control. They are a gardener's friend as they eat slugs and snails which destroy plants. They are also an important part of the food chain. Rats, foxes, crows, and hedgehogs eat them.

Frogs have longer legs than most toads, which help them to take long leaps.

What are their feet like?

A frog's hind feet are webbed to help it swim.

WHAT IS A CAECILIAN?

Caecilians are amphibians that look like small snakes or giant earthworms. They live hidden in the ground most of the time. Most species have smooth, dark skin. Their eyes are protected by skin, and they have two tentacles on their head.

DID YOU KNOW? Frogs catch live prey by darting out their long, sticky tongue.

Insects

Insects make up the largest group of creatures on Earth. Eight out of every 10 animals are insects. Some of the most common are bees, ants, beetles, flies, butterflies, crickets, dragonflies, and cockroaches.

What is an insect's body like?

It has three parts: a head, a thorax, and an abdomen. The head has a pair of antennae, eyes, and a mouth. The thorax supports the six legs and wings. The abdomen digests food and helps the insect breathe.

How do insects breathe?

They have little holes called spiracles on the sides of their thorax and abdomen. Air enters through these and then the oxygen is carried through the body by breathing tubes. The spiracles close if the insect is in water so it doesn't drown.

Are all creepy crawlies insects?

No! Spiders, centipedes, millipedes, and earthworms are not insects, as they do not have six legs.

Insects are the only invertebrates that can fly. Some, like this dragonfly, are skilled at turning, diving, and hovering.

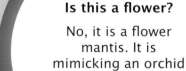

Insects keep the planet clear of some waste, such as dead bodies, decomposing plants, and even dung.

Is this a flower?

No, it is a flower mantis. It is mimicking an orchid so it can catch unsuspecting prey.

WHY DO WE NEED INSECTS?

So many of them are helpful to us. Butterflies, ants, bees, and wasps pollinate flowers and help to grow new plants. Some beetles eat dead animals or other insects. Grasshoppers lay so many eggs that if all of them were to hatch, they could devour our crops. This doesn't happen because other insects eat the grasshopper eggs.

Where are its six legs?

Its four back legs look like parts of the flower and its front legs are ready to strike.

DID YOU KNOW? Some grasshoppers can jump 20 times the length of their own body.

69

Types of mammal

Mammals all breathe air, and give birth to live young, which they feed with their milk. Some spend all their time in the ocean, and some can fly. Mammals might be huge or tiny, tree-climbers or burrowers, and sprinters or plodders. Take a look at some of the best-known groups of mammals.

Primates

Primates are a group of mammals that includes monkeys, apes, and humans. They have a large, highly developed brain that helps them to remember things and understand others. They usually have thumbs on both hands and feet that can be used for grasping.

Canines

The canine family includes dogs, wolves, foxes, coyotes, dingoes, and jackals. Dogs were probably the first animals to be domesticated by humans, but wild canines can still be found in every part of the world.

Bears

Bears are found on every continent except Antarctica. Those living in places with cold winters spend the season sleeping in a warm, cosy den.

DID YOU KNOW? Bears are really clever! They have the largest and most complex brains compared to other land mammals their size.

Big Cats

Most big cats have a long tail and a coat that is striped or spotted. They are highly territorial, with their own area that includes hunting grounds, dens, and water holes. They warn off other cats by marking their territory, usually by spraying urine or scratching trees.

Hoofed Animals

One group of mammals is identified by its feet. These animals are called ungulates and have hooves. Odd-toed ungulates include rhinoceroses, horses, and zebras. Even-toed ungulates include hippopotamuses, pigs, camels, giraffes, goats, and cattle.

Whales

Although they live in the ocean their whole lives, whales are mammals that give birth to live young and breathe with their lungs.

Monkeys

Monkeys belong to the group of mammals called primates, which also includes apes and humans. These species share some characteristics, such as narrow noses and five fingers and toes. However, many monkeys have tails, which apes and humans do not.

How many primate species are there?

There may be more than 500 species in the world. Small to medium-sized primates, such as lemurs and lorises, have long whiskers and excellent senses of smell and hearing. Most larger primates, including other monkeys and apes, have a flat face and poor sense of smell.

Tarsiers have enormous eyes, long feet, and are active at night. They are carnivorous, eating insects, birds, lizards, and snakes.

Baboons are Old World monkeys that live in Africa. They have a nose that points downward.

Why are monkeys called social animals?

Most species of monkey live in groups. The size of a group depends on how much food is available and if there are predators around. An important part of socializing is grooming, when monkeys run their hands through each other's fur to get rid of parasites.

Do monkeys make a noise?

Some species can be very noisy indeed! Those that live in groups use signs and calls to communicate. Some, like the African vervet monkey, use a different alarm call for each of their main predators, such as eagles, leopards, and snakes.

What are New World monkeys?

They are monkeys that live in Central and South America, like these capuchin monkeys. Old World monkeys live in Africa and Asia.

DID YOU KNOW? Howler monkeys can be heard up to 3 km (1.9 mi) away through the trees.

The spider monkey of Central and South America has a tail whose tip is so well developed, it acts like a fifth hand. Each tail-tip even has its own unique "fingerprint."

How are New World monkeys' tails different from Old World monkeys'?

New World monkeys have prehensile tails, which they can use to grasp things.

DO MONKEYS LIVE IN COLD PLACES?

The Japanese macaque, also known as the snow monkey, is one of the few primates that live in cold regions. They are found in the mountains of Honshu in Japan. They gather near hot springs to keep warm.

Apes

Apes are primates with long arms, a broad chest, and no tail. Early apes evolved several million years ago, long before humans. Gibbons, siamangs, and orang utans live in Asia, while gorillas, bonobos, and chimpanzees are African apes.

What does "great apes" mean?

Apes are sometimes subdivided into two groups according to their size. The biggest—gorillas, chimpanzees, bonobos, and orang utans—are called great apes. Gibbons and siamangs are sometimes called lesser apes.

Which ape is the biggest?

Gorillas are the largest of all. Adult males are about 1.8 m (6 ft) tall. Although they have been portrayed as aggressive, they are in reality shy, peaceful plant-eaters. They do not attack people unless provoked.

Which are the smallest apes?

Gibbons are smaller than other apes, and from a distance they look more like monkeys than apes. They live in pairs. Their skull and teeth, however, are more like those of an ape.

Gibbons swing through tree branches in a movement known as brachiation. They can swing around 15 m (50 ft) using their long arms.

The male siamang can inflate its throat pouch to make loud calls.

WHAT IS A BONOBO?

The bonobo is a species that looks very similar to the chimpanzee. They are the closest relatives to humans. They walk on two feet more than other apes. Today, they are found only in the forests of the Congo basin in Africa, and are in danger of becoming extinct.

Where do orang utans live?

On the islands of Sumatra and Borneo. They are the largest Asian apes.

What do they eat?

Orang utans are omnivores, eating both meat and plants. They often use tools to find or collect food.

DID YOU KNOW? Each evening, gorillas curl up and sleep in nests that they make using leaves and twigs.

Big cats

Big cats have large eyes, sharp teeth, excellent hearing, and powerful limbs with sharp claws. This group includes the lion, tiger, jaguar, and leopard.

How are big cats different from other cats?

Big cats are similar to our pet cats in many ways. However, only big cats can roar. In small cats, the hyoid bone (which connects the tongue to the roof of the mouth) is hard, while in big cats the hyoid is flexible, helping them open their mouths really wide and roar loudly.

The flexible hyoid bone of the big cats allows them to roar.

Do big cats have retractable claws ?

All big cats—except the cheetah—have claws which can be drawn into the paw when the cat is not using them. This prevents the cat from getting hurt while grooming.

Why do the eyes of a big cat glow in the night?

This is caused by a mirror-like layer in the eyes. It gathers even the faintest light and focuses it on an object, making it clearly visible to the cat.

What happens when a big cat kills its prey?

Their teeth cut through the skull or spinal cord, often killing the prey instantly. Smaller teeth help the cat scrape the meat off the bones.

IS THE CHEETAH A BIG CAT?

The cheetah is not actually a big cat, as it cannot roar. However, it has many other characteristics of a big cat. It is the fastest of all land animals, and can run at a speed of up to 110 km/h (70 mph) over a short distance.

Do leopards live in packs?

Adult leopards, like most other big cats, usually live by themselves except during the mating season.

DID YOU KNOW? Big cats are found in all continents except Australia and Antarctica.

77

Bears

Bears can be found in a wide range of habitats, including mountains and Arctic regions. There are eight species of bear—the spectacled bear, the sun bear, the giant panda, the Asiatic black bear, the American black bear, the brown bear, the sloth bear, and the polar bear.

What do bear species have in common?

Bears have a stocky body, powerful limbs, thick fur, and a short tail. They have an elongated head, rounded ears, and a long snout, with a keen sense of hearing and smell.

What do bears eat?

There are some differences in diet between species, but all bears except the polar bear are omnivorous. Their varied diet includes roots, nuts, fruit, berries, honey, caterpillars, and ants.

The giant panda eats bamboo leaves, stems, and shoots. It spends up to 14 hours a day just eating.

What is a grizzly bear?

It is the American name for a brown bear.

What does a bear use its claws for?

Each of a bear's four paws has five long, sharp claws. They use them to climb trees, open beehives and termite nests, dig for roots, and catch prey.

The Asiatic black bear is also known as the moon bear because of the white mark on its chest. It lives in the forests of Asia.

What kind of teeth do bears have?

Bear teeth are relatively small, and are mainly used as tools, and to defend themselves. The molars are broad and flat for shredding and grinding fruit, nuts, and berries.

WHICH IS THE LARGEST BEAR?

The polar bear is not only the largest bear but also the largest land carnivore. They can grow to a length of 2 m (7 ft) and weigh a massive 800 kg (1,760 lb). They prefer to eat meat, mostly seals and young walruses.

DID YOU KNOW? Polar bears are excellent swimmers and spend almost as much time in water as they do on land.

Canines

All canines have a keen sense of hearing and smell. As a result, they can locate prey a long way off. They are very determined hunters, willing to chase prey over long distances. Their long legs and ankle bones allow them to run fast and have a lot of stamina.

What makes them good hunters?

They have several sharp teeth used for killing, feeding, and defending themselves. They use their chisel-like incisors for cutting food and grooming. Next to them is a pair of dagger-shaped canine teeth for fighting and hunting. Their feet are small, and their toes have small but blunt claws. Canines can run very efficiently.

How do wolves hunt?

Timber wolves live and hunt in a pack. The wolf pack might follow its prey (such as a herd of elk) for days before it actually attacks. The wolves are looking for any animal that is weaker and might be a good target. By hunting together, wolves are able to prey on animals that are bigger than a wolf.

Why do wolves howl?

Howling is a popular method of communication for them. It helps pack members find each other even in thick forests or snow storms. It can be used to gather pack members at a specific location. It can also help a wolf lay claim to its territory and warn off rivals.

Wolf packs are closely knit and usually all members are related to one another, though distantly. The pack hunts and feeds together, though smaller family groups may sleep separately in dens that are close to one another.

What are painted wolves?

African wild dogs are sometimes known as "painted wolves" due to their patterned coats, which help them to camouflage in the Savannah.

DID YOU KNOW? A fennec fox's coat can repel sunlight in the day and conserve heat at night.

DO FOXES HUNT IN PACKS?

Foxes usually hunt alone. Some species, like the red fox, may live in small groups, with a male and female defending their territory. Sometimes, several female red foxes (usually a mother and her daughters) live in a group with a single male.

Who is in charge?

The pack is led by an alpha female who decides where to hunt, when to rest, and what they will hunt for.

The tiny fennec fox is the smallest member of the canine family. They are only around 65 cm (2 ft) from their ears to the tip of their tail. Their huge ears help get rid of excess heat in the desert.

Hoofed mammals

Many mammals walk on their toes rather than on the flat part of their foot. Often, their toenails are large and hard enough for them to walk on. These nails are called hooves and such animals are called hoofed animals, or ungulates. They can be divided into two groups: even-toed ungulates and odd-toed ungulates.

How many toes do they have?

A hippopotamus has four toes; a rhinoceros has three toes; deer, antelopes, camels, and llamas have two toes; and horses and zebras have just one toe, or hoof.

Are antelopes and deer related?

No, they aren't. Antelopes are more closely related to sheep and goats. They have pointed, hollow horns that are permanently on their head. Deer have branched antlers that they shed every year. These antlers are solid and bony. Only male deer grow antlers, while both male and female antelopes grow horns.

Do hippopotamuses sweat?

Common hippos do not have sweat glands. However, their pores secrete a reddish-pink fluid, which is often mistaken for blood. This fluid makes their skin look shiny and prevents it from cracking in the heat. A hippopotamus spends a large part of its day in shallow water and usually comes out only at night.

There are two species of camel. The Bactrian camel has two humps on its back. The Arabian camel, or dromedary, has only one hump.

Llamas, alpacas, vicuñas, and guanacos are found in the Andes mountains in South America. They are in the same family as camels and look similar, but without a hump.

WHY ARE TAPIRS UNUSUAL?

They have four toes on their front feet and only three toes on their hind feet! A tapir's splayed hooves help it get a grip on muddy ground. They are closely related to zebras and rhinos.

Are all rhinos the same species?

There are five species of rhinoceros in the world today. The white rhino (seen here) and black rhino are found in Africa. The Sumatran, Javan, and Indian rhinoceros all live in Asia.

What are rhinos like?

Rhinos have thick skin with folds. Their legs are short and they have a tiny tail. They are solitary animals that come together only during the mating season.

DID YOU KNOW? Indian rhinos have one horn, while African rhinos have two.

Other land mammals

Some mammals can't be grouped together. Elephants are bigger than any other animal on land and live only in Africa and Asia. Bats and anteaters don't follow the normal rules of mammals, and another group, marsupial mammals, are even more unusual.

How are African elephants different from Asian elephants?

African elephants are larger and have less hair. They have bigger, fan-shaped ears. Both males and females have tusks. Only male Asian elephants grow tusks.

What are an elephant's tusks?

They are simply elongated incisor teeth. A calf is born with a pair of incisors that are replaced within six to 12 months. The second set grows into tusks.

The giant anteater has no teeth, but it does have an extremely long tongue for lapping up ants and termites.

Do any mammals lay eggs?

Most mammals give birth to live young. However, the duck-billed platypus and the spiny anteater are mammals that lay eggs. They have a snout that looks like a beak, and no teeth.

WHAT ARE MARSUPIAL MAMMALS?

They are animals that carry their babies in a pouch. Their baby is born before it has finished developing, and it climbs into its mother's pouch until it is strong enough to move around on its own. Kangaroos, koalas, possums, and wombats are all marsupials.

How does an elephant use its trunk?

It uses it to grasp objects, pluck leaves, and carry heavy objects like logs. An elephant's trunk is a combination of its nose and upper lip.

Do elephants live alone?

African elephants live in herds with the oldest female in charge. They feed, bathe, and migrate together.

Whales

Whales are among the largest animals on the planet and can be found in all the world's oceans. They can be divided into two groups—toothed whales and baleen whales. Many of them migrate huge distances to find food or a place to breed. They have a layer of fat, called blubber, between their skin and flesh.

A whale's tail is divided into two parts, called flukes. While a fish flicks its tail sideways to swim, whales swim by moving their giant tail up and down.

How does a whale breathe?

They take in air through nostrils, just like other mammals. However, these nostrils, called blowholes, are found on top of their head. Once in a while, a whale comes to the surface and opens its blowhole to breathe. It blows out stale air, which condenses into droplets forming a fountain or spout.

What do whales eat?

They can be divided into two groups, depending on their preferred food. Toothed whales hunt for prey. Baleen whales feed on krill, plankton, and other tiny creatures in the water.

Do whales like to play?

Although they are big, whales can be playful. Sometimes, they pop their head above the surface and float motionless. This is known as logging. Some whales, such as humpbacks and orcas, leap right out of the water in an action known as breaching. Whales also stick their tail out of the water and splash around, which is called lob-tailing.

How do humpback whales feed?

Humpback whales are filter feeders. They gulp enormous mouthfuls of water and prey, then filter out the water with their baleen plates.

DID YOU KNOW? The blue whale is the largest animal to have ever lived. They are also the loudest animal on Earth!

A baleen whale has baleen instead of teeth. Baleen is made of keratin, the same substance that makes fingernails and hair. Blue whales, minke whales, bowhead whales, and right whales are all baleen whales.

Where can you find humpback whales?

Humpback whales live in both the northern hemisphere and the southern hemisphere. Both populations migrate from cold polar waters to warmer waters, but northern and southern humpback whales never meet each other.

DO THEY HAVE SHARP TEETH?

Toothed whales such as sperm whales, beluga whales, and orcas (killer whales) have small, sharp teeth in their jaws. These are used to kill a variety of prey, ranging from fish to seals and penguins.

Other marine mammals

One group of mammals is at home in the sea, but comes onto land at certain times. These are the pinnipeds—fin-footed animals that feed in the ocean but give birth out of the water. Seals, sea lions, and walruses are all pinnipeds.

How many species of seal are there?

There are 32 species altogether. These are divided into true seals and eared seals. True seals appear clumsy on land. Their flippers are no use for walking. Eared seals, including sea lions and fur seals (main picture), can rotate their rear flippers to help them move. As their name suggests, eared seals have tiny but visible ear flaps on the outside of their heads, while true seals do not.

Not all marine mammals are pinnipeds. Sea otters are in the same group of mammals as weasels and badgers.

HOW ARE WALRUSES DIFFERENT?

They are much bigger than seals. They inhabit the Arctic regions at the edge of the polar ice sheet. Their tusks are a pair of elongated upper canine teeth. They use them to defend themselves, and also as hooks to help them climb onto the ice.

Why are seals good swimmers?

They have a torpedo-shaped body that makes it easy to move through the water. They also have strong limbs shaped like paddles that help to propel them forward. Most seals are able to stay submerged and chase their prey for many minutes without breathing. In the water, they are a sleek, fast predator.

Dugongs and manatees are sirenians. These heavy, sausage-shaped mammals swim slowly near the shore and never leave the water.

How big are seals?

Seals range in size from 1 m (3 ft) to over 5 m (16 ft). The male southern elephant seal is the largest in the world. Galapagos fur seals and ringed seals are the smallest.

Do seals live together or alone?

Seals live in large colonies, often on remote islands. The colonies are divided into nurseries, for part-grown seals, and an area nearest the sea for adults.

DID YOU KNOW? Weddell seals have been known to stay underwater for over an hour.

89

What is the body made of?

Your body is a brilliant machine made up of cells. These cells form tissues, such as skin or bone. Tissues of different types form your organs, such as the liver, kidneys, or stomach. Medical specialists study our various body bits to help keep us healthy or heal us if something goes wrong.

On the outside

Your body is protected from the outside world by your skin, your nails, and even your hair. Fine hairs all over your body help to keep it warm. There are about 5 million hair follicles on the human body, plus another 100,000 or so on the head.

Bones and muscles

Without bones or muscles, your body would be floppy and squishy like a jellyfish! Bones and muscles work together to help you sit up straight, move around, eat your meals, and do all the things you enjoy doing.

The glands in your neck may swell if you are ill. Glands are part of the endocrine system.

Body systems

Organs and tissues work together in systems to perform your bodily functions. These systems include the nervous system and the muscular system, but also lesser-known ones such as the endocrine system (which makes hormones that act as chemical messengers around your body).

Reproduction

Males and females have different reproductive systems. The male organs allow him to fertilize an egg. The female organs produce the egg and then carry the growing baby and eventually allow her to give birth. Human babies are dependent on their parents or other adults for much longer than most other animals.

Falling sick

Harmful bacteria and viruses can make us ill with infections (such as a sore throat or upset stomach) or diseases (such as chickenpox, measles, or influenza). Our body has to fight off the germs to make us well again. A medic can prescribe drugs to help us get better.

On the outside

The human body is operated by sensitive organs that are kept safe inside the body. The parts that can be seen outside all have their own uses in helping us to function and keeping us safe and healthy.

What is skin for?

The skin holds all our internal organs together and protects our insides from injury. It is itself the largest organ of the body. When the skin is broken, germs can attack us. Sweat glands under the skin get rid of poisons that could otherwise harm us.

Hair grows from a tiny opening in the skin called a follicle. It is made of a protein called keratin.

What do our feet do?

They help us to balance and move. The human foot is made of the heel, instep, sole, ball, and toes. The toes help us balance and push the foot off the ground with each step. The arch and heel absorb the shock of hitting the ground.

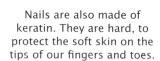

Nails are also made of keratin. They are hard, to protect the soft skin on the tips of our fingers and toes.

Why do we need hands?

The human hand has five digits: four fingers and one thumb. The thumb helps us grip things better. We can move and bend our fingers because each is made up of three separate bones. The thumb has only two bones so is less flexible.

WHAT HAPPENS WHEN WE HURT OURSELVES?

Our skin is being replaced all the time. New skin grows from below. On average, almost all of our skin is replaced every month. It is because skin replaces itself that cuts can heal so quickly.

What is skin made of?

It has layers of cells that contain nerves, blood vessels, hair follicles, and glands.

How much skin do we have?

An adult has more than 2 sq m (20 sq ft) of skin. This is almost the size of a bed sheet!

DID YOU KNOW? Every minute, we lose 30,000–40,000 dead skin cells, which are replaced by new ones.

Bones and muscles

The skeleton is like a scaffolding of bones inside us. It allows us to sit, stand, walk, run, and do everything else that we do. It gives our body a definite shape, supports our muscles, and protects our internal organs.

Some parts of our bodies are made of cartilage instead of bone. It is tough and rubbery.

How many bones do we have?

A human baby is born with 270 bones. Some of these join together as we grow, and by the time we are adults, we have only 206 bones.

What are muscles?

They are tissues that can contract and return to their normal length. A muscle is made of thread-like proteins and is connected to bones, skin, cartilage, or ligaments. Involuntary muscles move on their own, like the cardiac muscles in our hearts.

How do muscles and bones work together?

Most muscles are connected to bones to help you move. They form your musculoskeletal system, which also relies on connective tissue. Muscles are connected to bones by tendons. Bones are connected to other bones by ligaments.

ARE THERE DIFFERENT TYPES OF BONES?

Yes, there are four kinds, depending on their shape. Long bones are long and thin, short bones have a cubed shape, and flat bones have a broad, flat surface. Any bones with a different shape from these are called irregular bones.

What is bone marrow?

It is the soft tissue inside bones that produces blood cells.

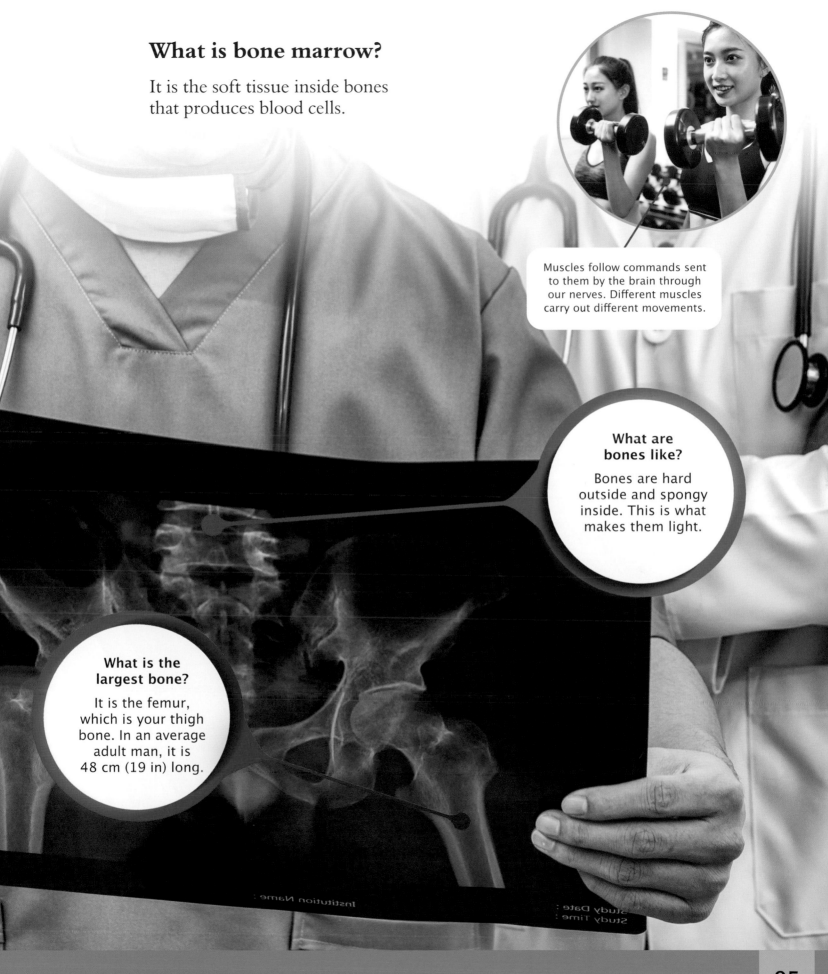

Muscles follow commands sent to them by the brain through our nerves. Different muscles carry out different movements.

What are bones like?

Bones are hard outside and spongy inside. This is what makes them light.

What is the largest bone?

It is the femur, which is your thigh bone. In an average adult man, it is 48 cm (19 in) long.

DID YOU KNOW? We have more facial muscles than any other animal.

95

The digestive system

What happens to the food we eat? Where does it go, and how does our body gain energy from it? Food goes through an incredible journey from the moment we take a bite. This process is called digestion and involves several organs in the body.

Why is it important to chew food?

The more we chew, the easier it is for our body to digest food. As we chew, the mouth releases saliva that moistens the food so it passes through the digestive system without scraping any of the organs.

Most of our energy comes from carbohydrates such as grains, potatoes, vegetables, and fruit.

Some teeth are used for biting and tearing food, others help to grind it up.

How long does it take to get to the stomach?

Food takes about eight seconds to travel down the food pipe from the mouth to the stomach.

What happens after we swallow?

The food moves down to the stomach, where it is churned and broken into tinier pieces. Stomach acid kills harmful bacteria, while other chemicals speed up digestion. Water, sugar, and salt are filtered into the blood through the stomach walls.

WHAT HAPPENS TO UNDIGESTED FOOD?

It moves through the small intestine into the large intestine, where any water is absorbed. Bacteria change the waste material into poop.

What does the small intestine do?

Undigested food, called chyme, passes from the stomach into the small intestine for further digestion. Small finger-like projections in the intestine, called villi, pass nutrients into the bloodstream.

How long does food take to digest?

Most of the food that we eat takes 20–30 hours to travel through our digestive system. That means what we eat today will "reappear" tomorrow.

DID YOU KNOW? The stomach can stretch to twice its empty size when filled with food.

97

The heart and circulation

The heart is a muscle that pumps blood to every part of our body. It is inside our ribcage, a little to the left-hand side of our chest. Blood carries oxygen and nutrients that the body needs. It also carries away waste. This movement of the blood is called circulation.

What is the circulatory system?

The heart, the lungs, and blood vessels are part of the circulatory system. Humans have about 100,000 km (62,000 mi) of blood vessels in their body. That's enough to circle the Earth two and a half times!

What types of blood vessels are there?

Blood vessels are made up of arteries, veins, and capillaries. Arteries carry blood away from the heart. Veins bring blood back to the heart. Capillaries connect arteries to veins.

What does the circulatory system do?

Your lungs absorb oxygen from the air you breathe and transfer it into your blood. Your heart then pumps the oxygenated blood all around your body.

Breathing out gets rid of the carbon dioxide from our lungs.

People have different types of blood, so it has been divided into four groups: A, B, AB, and O.

How many times does the heart beat?

It beats about 100,000 times in one day. It begins before a child is born and does not stop beating until the person dies.

Why does our heart beat?

It beats because it is pumping blood. Normally it beats 72 times in a minute. It beats faster during exercise.

HOW IS THE HEART STRUCTURED?

The heart has four chambers, two on each side, one above the other. A wall of muscle separates the left and right sides.

DID YOU KNOW? Your heart is about the same size as your fist.

The nervous system

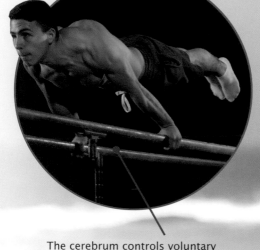

The brain, millions of nerves, and the spinal cord make up the central nervous system of the human body. All the information gathered by sense organs like the eyes, ears, nose, tongue, and skin is processed in the brain.

What is the brain?

It is an organ inside the skull that controls our feelings, movements, skills, and every function necessary to live. It is divided into three major parts. These are the cerebrum, the cerebellum, and the brainstem.

What does the brainstem do?

It connects the rest of the brain to the spinal cord, which runs down the neck and back. It controls involuntary muscles that work without us thinking about it, like the heart, the lungs, and the stomach.

The cerebrum controls voluntary muscles that allow us to dance, jump, do gymnastics, and solve puzzles.

When light enters our eyes, special nerves inside the eyes carry a message to our brains.

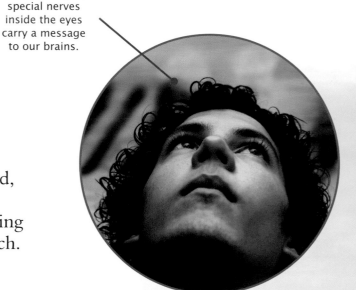

WHERE DOES INTELLIGENCE COME FROM?

The cerebrum, which makes up 85 percent of the brain, is responsible for our intelligence. It operates voluntary muscles that we have control over. It also stores information, which we call memory.

Why is smell useful?

It helps us to examine the environment around us and warns us in case of potential dangers like smoke. It also helps us to taste food and work out whether it is bad.

Where does the brain get information from?

Basic information comes from the sense organs, helping us to see, hear, taste, feel, smell, and react.

What do nerves do?

They help to deliver messages from the spine to other body parts. Thirty-one pairs of spinal nerves connect the spinal cord to the rest of the body.

Why is the cerebellum called the "little brain"?

Located just below the cerebrum, it is sometimes called the "little brain" because it is only one eighth the size. The cerebellum controls balance and tells the muscles how to move.

Reproduction and birth

Like all other living creatures, human beings reproduce. We are mammals, so we give birth to live children. The growth period, when a fertilized egg grows inside the mother's womb, is called pregnancy.

When can a human being reproduce?

It takes many years before a human can reproduce. The body of a child goes through changes between the ages of around eight and 15. This period is called puberty and it makes a person ready to produce children.

What are male reproductive organs?

Male reproductive organs are outside the body. They include the penis, and a pair of testes inside a cover called the scrotum. The testes produce sperm and the male hormone testosterone.

What are female reproductive organs?

The female reproductive system is inside the body, in the pelvic region. It is made up of two ovaries, a uterus, two fallopian tubes, the cervix, and the vagina. The ovaries make eggs, which join with a male's sperm to produce a baby.

Sometimes, two babies develop from the same sperm and egg. They are called identical twins and look almost exactly the same.

Crying is a newborn baby's main form of communication. It shows that it is tired, hungry, sick, hot, cold, or wants attention.

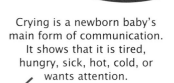

How long does it take for a baby to grow?

The egg grows inside the mother's womb for about 40 weeks.

HOW IS AN EGG FERTILIZED?

Each of us starts from a tiny cell. Millions of sperm cells are suspended in a mixture called semen. One sperm cell from the father joins an egg cell from the mother. The egg then attaches itself to the uterus wall and prepares itself for growth.

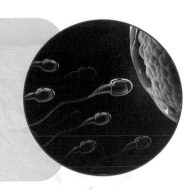

How does the baby get food?

During pregnancy, the growing baby gets food and blood from the mother through the umbilical cord attached to its belly button.

DID YOU KNOW? The sperm cell carries information that determines the sex of the baby.

103

Falling sick

When we feel good and the body and the mind are working as they should, we are in good health. When we have trouble with any part of our body, we usually fall ill. We may catch germs and get sick. Some diseases can even kill us.

Why do people fall ill?

The human body is made up of many organs. If even one of these organs does not do the work it is supposed to do, we can fall ill. To work well, the body needs the right kind of food in the right quantities. It also needs exercise and a clean environment.

How does exercise help?

Physical activity makes us breathe deeply, and our lungs get more oxygen. It keeps the heart healthy and our weight in check.

Physical activity keeps our body and mind healthy. It builds up muscles and strengthens bones.

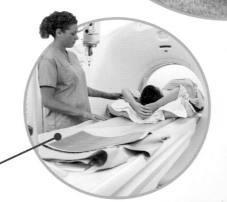

Modern technology can make it easier for specialists to find out if something is wrong with us.

WHAT FOOD DOES THE BODY NEED?

The body works best when it is fed a balanced diet with food from the five basic food groups. These are carbohydrates, vitamins, minerals, proteins, and fatty acids. A varied diet with grains, beans, pulses, nuts, and vegetables gives us a lot of these nutrients.

How long do humans live?

The average life span around the world is 70.5 years and is increasing. Following a healthy lifestyle can slow the physical effects of getting older.

What do germs do?

Germs are tiny creatures that can only be seen through a microscope. They cause infections and diseases.

What happens when we get older?

Our cells can divide to replace dead cells, but not forever. The effects, such as wrinkled skin, whitening hair, worsening sight and hearing, and painful joints, are felt in old age.

DID YOU KNOW? Humans are the longest living of all land mammals.

105

What can we learn from science?

For thousands of years, people observed the world around them and put forward theories about the way the world works. Through time, the development of scientific method has allowed us to record and test our theories to gain a better understanding of nature, our bodies and disease, and the universe we live in.

Matter

Everything you can see, touch, or smell is made up of matter. Matter is made of basic substances called elements. Oxygen, iron, gold, and uranium are all elements. These elements can be combined to form mixtures or compounds, and are in all the things around us.

Light and sound

Both light and sound are forms of energy that travel as waves. They behave in different ways, though. Light can travel through a vacuum, while sound cannot. Sound has to travel through a solid, liquid, or gas.

Heat

We use heat energy every day. Electrical energy is converted into heat energy in appliances such as hair dryers, toasters, and ovens. Our bodies get heat energy from the food we eat. If your body gets too cold, it works more slowly. Even small changes in body temperature can make us feel ill.

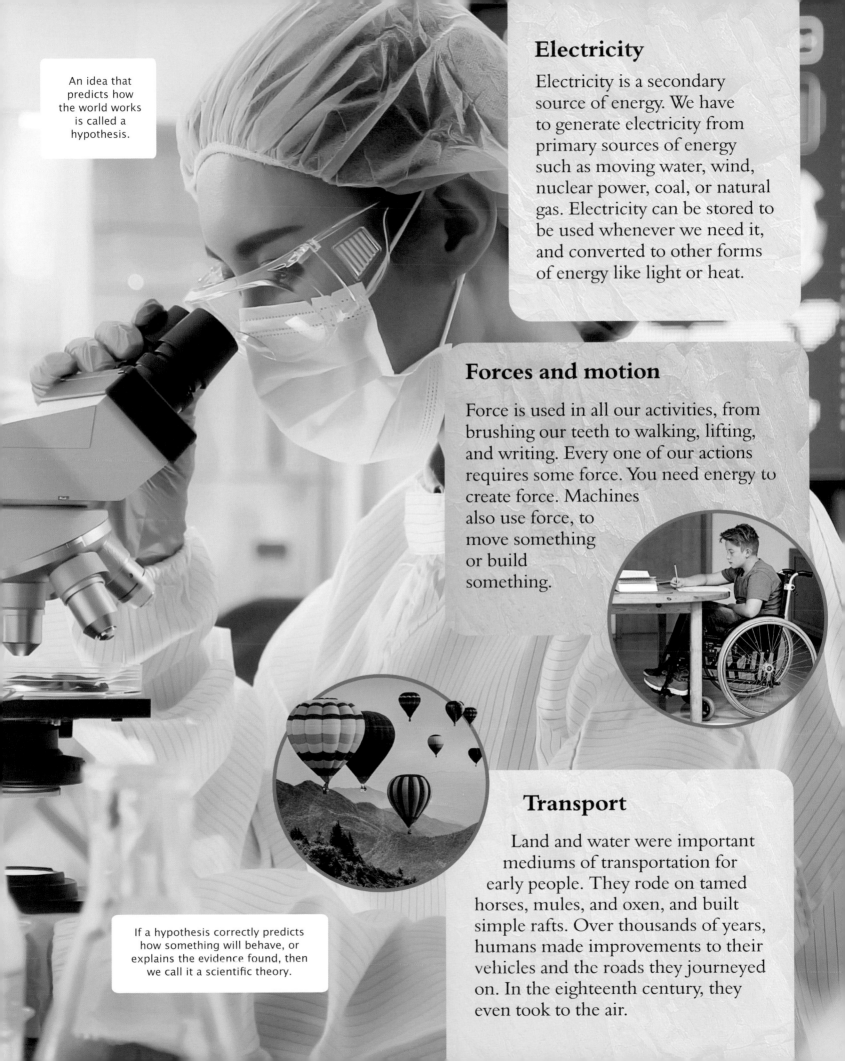

An idea that predicts how the world works is called a hypothesis.

Electricity

Electricity is a secondary source of energy. We have to generate electricity from primary sources of energy such as moving water, wind, nuclear power, coal, or natural gas. Electricity can be stored to be used whenever we need it, and converted to other forms of energy like light or heat.

Forces and motion

Force is used in all our activities, from brushing our teeth to walking, lifting, and writing. Every one of our actions requires some force. You need energy to create force. Machines also use force, to move something or build something.

If a hypothesis correctly predicts how something will behave, or explains the evidence found, then we call it a scientific theory.

Transport

Land and water were important mediums of transportation for early people. They rode on tamed horses, mules, and oxen, and built simple rafts. Over thousands of years, humans made improvements to their vehicles and the roads they journeyed on. In the eighteenth century, they even took to the air.

Matter

Everything around us is matter. Anything that occupies space and has weight is matter. It is made up of atoms and molecules. It takes three main forms, which are solid, liquid, and gas. All matter can change from one of these forms to another.

When some gases become very hot, they turn to plasma and glow, like these neon signs. Plasma is a fourth state of matter.

What does matter look like?

It is found in different forms and shapes. It can be as huge as a mountain or as tiny as sand. It can be hard like diamond, or as soft as silk.

What is matter made of?

The tiniest part of all matter is an atom. Several atoms form a molecule. Matter in solid state gets its shape because the atoms are packed close and tight. In the liquid state, atoms are more loosely packed. In the gas state, the atoms are even more spread out.

How does matter change state?

Solid, liquid, and gas are interchangeable by adding or taking away heat energy. The chemical properties of an element stay the same in all three states.

The Northern lights are an example of plasma occurring in nature. Stars also have plasma in them.

What is a compound?

Matter is made up of elements. Each element is made up of a single substance, such as oxygen or iron. If you combine two or more elements, you will get a compound. For example, if you heat carbon and oxygen, it will form carbon dioxide, which is a compound.

WHAT ARE CHEMICAL REACTIONS?

Sometimes, adding or taking away energy causes a chemical reaction that cannot be reversed. For example, when you heat bread, it turns brown and then black. It has been through an irreversible chemical reaction.

What forms does water take?

Water can be found in three forms, or states. These are ice (solid), water (liquid), and steam (gas).

DID YOU KNOW? A human hair is as wide as 1 million carbon atoms.

109

Light

Without light, we would not be able to see the beautiful world around us, and it wouldn't even exist. Light is essential for life to thrive on this planet. Animals and humans depend on plants for their food. Plants make their own food, but they cannot do so without light.

What is light?

Light is a form of energy. It is produced by both natural and artificial sources. A light source is any object that gives off light, such as the Sun, a candle, or an electric bulb.

Does light always travel in a straight line?

It does, unless a solid object is placed in its path. If the object is transparent, the light goes through it, but its direction is altered slightly.

Light bends around the edges of a solid object, creating a shadow. Solids are "opaque," as light does not pass through them.

Why can't we see objects on the other side of a wall?

We are able to see an object when light bounces off it and reaches our eyes. However, solid objects like walls block the light from passing through to the other side. Instead, the light hits the wall and bounces back. We can see the wall, but not the objects on the other side.

WHAT DO RAINBOWS HAVE TO DO WITH LIGHT?

Light waves are made up of all the different shades of the rainbow: red, orange, yellow, green, blue, indigo, and violet. They travel at different speeds, which means they reach our eyes at different times. When they are all combined, they appear white.

Why is the sky blue?

All light travels in little wiggles called waves. When sunlight reaches Earth's atmosphere, it scatters in different directions. Blue light travels in shorter waves, and so reaches our eyes before any other shade.

How long does it take for sunlight to travel to Earth?

Light from the Sun takes about eight minutes to reach us on Earth. It travels at an incredible speed of around 300,000 km (186,000 mi) per second. Nothing in the universe travels faster than that!

Light rays hit the surface of a mirror and bounce back so your eyes see the reflected image.

DID YOU KNOW? Rainbows happen when sunlight reflects off water, sending the waves in different directions.

Sound

Sound is a form of energy that is transferred by pressure waves in air or through other materials. These waves can be picked up by the ear, which is how we hear sounds. But there are many sounds around us that our ears do not pick up, and so we do not hear them.

How does sound move?

When something moves through the air, it disturbs the molecules of gas in the air around it. The air vibrates or moves back and forth. This vibration is heard as sound. Sound can also travel through water or solids, but not as easily as it does through air. This is why sounds might be muffled underwater, or if you hear them through a wall.

How fast does sound travel?

It travels much slower than light. Light travels at nearly 300,000 km (186,000 mi) per second and sound travels at around 8 km (5 mi) per second. That is why we see lightning before we hear thunder.

How do people speak?
We have vocal cords which produce sound. When air passes between them, they vibrate and make a sound.

All animals that can produce sound have vocal cords, except birds which make sound through a bony ring called a syrinx.

WHAT IS A SONIC BOOM?

When an aircraft flies faster than the speed of sound, it is hitting the sound waves in front before those waves have moved away. Successive waves get mixed up, creating a loud boom, like a thunderclap, called a sonic boom.

What is an echo?

Sound waves can be reflected off any reasonably flat surface, such as a cliff, high wall, or mountain. At the right distance from you, a sound you make hits the surface and comes back to you as an echo.

A young person can hear a wider range of sounds than an older person.

Why are some sounds louder than others?

A bigger vibration makes a louder sound. Since sound travels in waves, it gets weaker the farther it travels. That is why your voice cannot be heard beyond a certain distance.

DID YOU KNOW? Dogs have amazing hearing, and can detect sounds that are too high-pitched for humans to hear.

113

Heat

Heat is a form of energy that is created by atoms moving. It is also known as thermal energy. Many types of energy (light, chemical, sound, and nuclear) can be converted into heat energy by increasing the speed of the atoms in the object that is producing the energy.

When sunlight touches a solar cell, it causes a chemical reaction and electricity is generated. This is called solar power.

Where do we find heat?

The largest heat source in nature is the Sun. It is a burning ball of gas whose average surface temperature is 6,000°C (10,800°F), about 400 times the average surface temperature on Earth.

How is heat measured?

On Earth, heat can be measured using a thermometer. This is a glass tube that ends in a bulb containing liquid (often ethanol). The liquid heats up and expands, making it rise up the tube. The tube has numbers on it to measure the temperature.

Why do we cook food?

Cooking uses heat to convert raw food into something that is digested more easily. The heat creates chemical changes in the food.

How is heat transferred?

Heat moves from one thing to another by conduction (when two substances are close to each other), convection (when currents move through liquids and gas), and radiation (the transfer of heat in straight lines, like the rays of the Sun).

WHAT IS BOILING POINT?

It is the temperature at which a substance changes from liquid to gas. When you boil water, heat energy makes the molecules in the water move faster. To move fast, the molecules need more space, so they expand.

How can I light a fire?

Rubbing two things together causes friction, which creates heat. Striking a match on a matchbox uses friction to make the chemicals on the match head catch fire.

Melting point is the temperature at which a substance changes from a solid to a liquid.

DID YOU KNOW? Even cold things have some heat energy because their atoms move (albeit slowly).

Electricity

Electricity is used for lighting and heating or cooling our homes. It runs machines to wash clothes and dishes, and to cook. It brings us information through computers and television. The electricity used in our towns and cities is generated in power stations.

Who discovered electricity?

The ancient Greeks knew that electricity could be produced by rubbing two pieces of felt together. In 1752, Benjamin Franklin proved that lightning was created by electric charges.

What is electricity?

At the middle of an atom is a nucleus, made of protons and neutrons. Electrons spin around the nucleus, carrying a negative charge. When electrons pass from one atom to the next, it creates an electrical current.

What substances conduct electricity?

Materials such as copper and silver have low resistance, and are good conductors. Resistance is measured in ohms and is a material's opposition to the flow of electric current through it.

Can electricity be stored?

Yes, it can be kept in a battery and used when it is needed.

The human body has a continuous flow of electric current through our nerve cells. That is how they convey messages, such as pain, to our brain.

What uses most electricity?

Industry consumes huge amounts, but in the home, the biggest energy use is for heating or air conditioning.

DOES MY BRAIN USE ELECTRICITY?

The human brain runs on about as much power as a 10-watt lightbulb. The neurons in your brain use electricity to communicate with each other.

Static electricity is created when you rub against a charged surface. The extra electrons move and a tiny spark of electricity is made.

How is electricity measured?

Current (the number of charged electrons flowing between two points) is measured in amps. Voltage (the measure of the strength of an electric current) is measured in volts.

Magnets

Any object that attracts metals such as iron, cobalt, nickel, or steel to itself is a magnet. A magnet can push away (repel) other magnets. Some magnets, like iron, are very strong, while others are weaker.

How did people first use magnets?

The magnet was discovered in China as early as 200 BCE. Around this time, people found out that magnets could be used to show directions like north and south.

What is a lodestone?

It is the most magnetic substance on Earth. Sailors once used lodestone to navigate. In the sixteenth century, it was discovered that a piece of iron could take on the properties of a lodestone if you rubbed it with lodestone. Scientists were then able to create many more magnets.

Where are magnets used?

Most electrical appliances, from hair dryers to refrigerators, have a magnet of some sort inside. Many credit cards have magnetic strips that contain encrypted information.

Magnets are used for recycling, to help sort steel objects from other metals.

HOW CAN MAGNETS HELP OUR HEALTH?

An MRI scanner uses radio waves and a powerful magnet to create pictures of the inside of our body. It can be helpful in diagnosing diseases such as cancer.

What are the poles of a magnet?

Just as the Earth has a north and south pole, so does a magnet. The north pole of a magnet will point toward the Earth's north pole. This is how compasses know to point north.

A magnetic material in touch with a magnet starts to behave like a magnet itself. That's how these metal nuts are sticking to each other.

Do the poles ever change?

Yes. The Earth's magnetic poles shift periodically. The needle of a compass always points to the current magnetic pole.

DID YOU KNOW? If you cut a large magnet into tiny pieces, each piece will still be a magnet.

Forces and motion

Force can change the state of an object. If an object is stationary, force can get it to move. Once it is moving, force can make the object accelerate or pick up speed. Force can also slow or stop a moving object.

What forces are there?

There are many different forces. Gravity, thrust, inertia, friction, torque, and air resistance are all examples. An applied force is one that is applied to an object by a person or by another object. This is what makes a skateboard move forward when you stand on it and push with your other foot.

What is gravitational force?

It is a force that draws everything around it toward a certain point. Earth's gravity draws everything within its atmosphere down toward the middle of the Earth. It keeps us on the ground.

What is inertia?

An object will carry on doing the same thing, whether it is at rest or moving, unless a force acts on it to change that. This is called inertia. Your phone sits on the table until you push it. This is called inertia of rest. Then, with the force of your finger, it moves until it meets another force that stops it. This is called inertia of motion.

WHAT ARE BALANCED FORCES?

Sometimes, the effect of one force is cancelled out by another. In a tug of war, one team wins by exerting more force. If the forces are balanced, the two teams don't move.

What is thrust?

Thrust is a force that increases the velocity of an object. Velocity is speed in a particular direction.

Spring force can be found in elastic materials. It is what makes a rubber band ping and a trampoline bounce.

What is friction?

When an object moves, a force called friction will pull in the opposite direction. Friction is the force that stops a moving object, like a skateboard, from moving forever without stopping.

DID YOU KNOW? Magnetic, electrical, and gravitational forces all act at a distance. They don't need contact between objects.

Communications

Connecting with other people no longer just means meeting for coffee, listening to the radio, or making a quick phone call. People now send messages in an instant, and keep in touch with social media and video conferencing. We also share information via TV and millions of web sites.

What is telecommunication?

It is the ability to communicate and exchange information over long distances.

Who invented the internet?

No single person came up with the idea, or how to make it work. It was developed in the 1960s to allow US government computers to communicate with each other.

Does my phone keep me awake?

Computer and phone screens emit blue light, which has very short, high-energy waves. If you spend too much time before bed looking at a screen, your brain will be fooled into thinking it is daytime, and your sleep cycle is likely to be disrupted.

The internet allows millions of people all over the world to work from home. They can talk to their coworkers using video conferencing software.

How do we watch live events?

Satellites are used to transmit footage of live events all around the world in real time, as they are happening.

WHAT IS IOT?

It is short for Internet of Things, and describes all devices that can be connected in your home or in the workplace. Kitchen appliances, lights, heating, even vehicles and toys can become smart devices.

Wearable technology such as a smart watch allows people to communicate more easily than ever.

How has TV developed through the decades?

TV broadcasts were in black and white until the 1960s. Cable TV appeared in the 1970s, and high definition in the late 1990s.

When was television invented?

Scottish engineer John Logie Baird is credited with giving the world's first demonstration of television in 1927. The first transatlantic transmission took place in 1928.

DID YOU KNOW? More than half of the world's population uses the internet regularly.

123

Transportation

The earliest travel was on land. At first, people walked, then tamed animals for travel. Gradually, they made themselves more comfortable, making carts and carriages. Modern transport includes bicycles, cars, and trains, as well as boats and planes.

What were the first boats like?

They were probably rafts or planks of wood. The earliest boat found dates back to 6300 BCE and was a hollowed-out tree trunk, also called a dugout. Around 4000 BCE, the Egyptians made long narrow boats powered by many oarsmen.

Electric cars don't use polluting fossil fuels, and have lower emissions than conventional cars.

When did roads improve?

People needed roads to trade and to conquer new lands. The Romans were the first to make all-weather roads. They dug road beds and filled them with crushed stone, and added paving stones on the busier routes.

Where were the first railroads built?

They were built in Germany around 1550. Horses pulled wagons along wooden rails and brought minerals out of mines. After the Industrial Revolution, rails were made of iron and so were the wheels. The development of the steam engine made rail transport easily available to carry people and goods over long distances.

Who first flew in a powered aircraft?

Brothers Orville and Wilbur Wright designed and constructed the first heavier-than-air plane. Their first flight took place in 1903.

Cycling is a non-polluting way to travel that improves fitness levels and won't get you stuck in a traffic jam!

What is a jet plane?

Jet engines fly by burning fuel, which produces enough hot gas to push the plane through the air. Jet planes were used extensively during World War II and these days they make air travel possible for millions of people.

WHAT IS A SUBMARINE?

It is a ship that can be entirely submerged underwater. Its sleek shape allows it to move quickly. Modern submarines can stay underwater for several months.

DID YOU KNOW? German inventor Carl Benz is credited with inventing the first car in 1886.

Glossary

AMPHIBIAN
An animal that lives in water and breathes through gills when young, but develops lungs for breathing air and can live on land as an adult.

ATOM
The smallest unit of an element.

BACTERIUM (pl. BACTERIA)
Tiny living thing with one cell.

BALEEN
A flexible keratin plate inside the mouth of some whales, which filters plankton from the water.

CARBOHYDRATE
One of a group of substances, which includes glucose, starch, and cellulose, that can be broken down to release energy in the body.

CARDIAC
Relating to the heart.

CARNIVORE
An animal that eats meat.

CARTILAGE
The soft substance that cushions bone ends in joints, and provides flexibility and support.

CELL
The smallest unit of a living body.

CEREBELLUM
The part of the brain that controls the body's sense of balance and coordination.

CEREBRUM
The largest part of the brain, divided into two hemispheres.

CLIMATE
The usual weather in a region, year after year.

COMPOUND
A form of matter made up of elements bound together by chemical bonds.

CONVECTION
The process that moves heat around in a liquid or gas as hot areas expand and rise, and cold ones sink.

CRUST
The hard, rocky outer layer of Earth.

DIGESTION
The breakdown of molecules in food into simple nutrients that can be absorbed into the bloodstream.

ELECTRICITY
A flow of electric charge from one place to another. It can be harnessed to do work.

ELEMENT
A substance that is made entirely from one type of atom. The 118 elements found so far are listed in the periodic table.

ENERGY
What allows us to do work. It comes in many forms, including heat, light, electricity, and nuclear.

EQUATOR
An imaginary line around Earth's middle, dividing it into northern and southern halves.

FORCE
A push or pull on another object that changes its movement.

FRICTION
A force between moving objects, where their surfaces rub against each other, slowing them down.

GAS
A phase of matter in which atoms or molecules are widely separated and move freely.

GLAND
An organ that releases a chemical substance, such as hormones or sweat, into or out of the body.

GLOBAL WARMING
Rising world temperatures caused mainly by human activities.

GRAVITY
A force that draws objects that have mass toward each other.

HERBIVORE
An animal that eats plants.

HORMONE
A chemical messenger made by an endocrine gland that is carried in the bloodstream to its target tissue or organ.

INVERTEBRATE
An animal without a backbone, such as a crab, squid, or insect.

KERATIN
A tough, waterproof protein found in hair, nails, and the epidermis (upper layer of skin).

LAVA
Hot, molten rock that has erupted from a volcano or fissure vent.

LIGHT WAVE
An electromagnetic wave emitted or reflected from most objects. Our eyes use light to see the objects that surround us.

LIQUID
A phase of matter in which atoms or molecules are loosely bound together but can move freely.

MAGMA
Hot, molten rock inside the Earth.

MAGNETIC FIELD
A form of electromagnetism created around, and felt by, electrical conductors and metals with certain properties.

MAMMAL
An animal that grows hair at some point in its life and feeds its young on milk, such as a whale or human.

MARROW
The soft tissue inside sections of large bone where new blood cells are produced.

MARSUPIAL
A mammal that gives birth to underdeveloped young that carry on growing in a pouch on their mother's belly.

MATTER
Anything that has mass and occupies space.

METEORITE
A piece of rock or metal that has fallen to Earth from space.

MOLECULE
The smallest unit of a compound, made up of two or more atoms bonded together.

NUTRIENT
A substance used by a living organism to survive, grow, and reproduce.

OMNIVORE
An animal that eats plants and meat.

ORGAN
A collection of tissues in a complex living thing (usually an animal) that carries out a special function to help the organism survive.

PREDATOR
An animal that hunts other animals.

PREY
An animal that is killed by another animal for food.

PRIMATE
A mammal with a large brain, flexible hands and feet, and good eyesight. The group includes humans, apes, monkeys, and lemurs.

PROTEIN
A molecule made up of amino acids that is a structural component of body tissue.

REPTILE
An animal with dry, scaly skin that lays eggs on land.

ROCK
A solid material found in nature, made up of a mix of minerals.

SOLID
A phase of matter in which atoms or molecules are tightly bound together and cannot move freely.

SPECIES
A group of living things with similar characteristics, which can breed with each other.

STAR
A huge ball of gas that produces energy, forcing small atomic nuclei together to form larger ones.

STATE OF MATTER
One of the main, distinct conditions in which matter exists, usually solid, liquid, or gas.

SUN
The star around which Earth orbits.

SYSTEM
A group of linked organs, such as those in the digestive system, that work together to do a task.

TECTONICS
The very slow movement and rearrangement of blocks of Earth's outer rocky crust, which cause volcanoes and earthquakes.

TISSUE
A collection of cells that carries out a function in a living organism.

UNGULATE
A mammal with four legs and hooves.

UNIVERSE
All existing matter, energy, and space.

VERTEBRATE
An animal that has a backbone.

VIRUS
A tiny organism that cannot grow or reproduce unless it is inside the cell of another organism.

WAVE
A moving disturbance that carries energy from one place to another.

Index